A Concise Russian Review Grammar

A Concise
Russian Review
Grammar with exercises

ROGER W. PHILLIPS

The University of Wisconsin Press

Published 1974
The University of Wisconsin Press
Box 1379
Madison, Wisconsin 53701

The University of Wisconsin Press, Ltd.
70 Great Russell Street, London

First printing

Printed in the United States of America
Malloy Lithographing, Inc., Ann Arbor, Michigan

ISBN 0-299-06544-8; LC 73-15260

PREFACE

This work is the product of twelve years' experience in teaching Russian grammar at the college level to students of widely varied background and ability. Over these years I have noted that students in the more elementary stages of Russian have two things in common. They seem to be intimidated by large amounts of material, either in grammar or exercises; and in the break between the first and second years, which usually means the summer months, they have a strong tendency to forget much of what they have learned.

This little book is intended to meet a definite need: to bridge the gap between the bulk of grammar the student is usually confronted with in his first year (especially toward the end, when the pace accelerates and too many things are crowded in) and the perhaps equally great body of advanced work in reading, composition, and conversation that looms before him. Digestion and assimilation of what has already been studied are necessary before he can profitably go on and make it through what is all too often a period of consternation and confusion.

To this end, the present work goes back over, although in a different form, the essential grammar the student was exposed to in his first year. It does not take up where the introductory textbook left off, with little or no overlap, but presents the same material, in a handier, more concise form. Повторе́нье--мать уче́нья, as the familiar proverb has it, and this is nowhere more true than in the learning of a language. I have adopted a "troubleshooting" approach to grammar here, consistently pointing out those mistakes the average-to-good student, and even the superior student on occasion, is likely to make-- errors ranging from the absent-minded type (e.g., кто вы зна́ете, who(m) do you know; где вы идёте, where are you going) through those indicating a more serious deficiency of knowledge (e.g. Ива́на дом, Ivan's house; я жду для него́, I'm waiting for him; он идёт к ба́нку, he is going to the bank; я холо́дный, I'm cold), to those involving more complicated problems of grammar and syntax (e.g. я хочу́ его́ прийти́, I want him to come; я начина́ю написа́ть письмо́, I am beginning to write a letter; он не говори́т с кем-нибудь, he isn't talking with anyone).

It should be emphasized that this work is not a reference grammar, nor does it make any pretensions to being "complete." The grammatical explanations are not intended to be thorough discussions followed by exhaustive examples. They are chiefly reminders to the student of what he is already supposed to know. If the book does not aim at completeness, however, it does try to achieve a certain roundness. Undoubtedly it will contain some material to which many students may not yet have been exposed, but which must nevertheless be considered essential; a good example of this is the usage of the pronoun то in such a sentence as я ду́мал о том, как игра́ ко́нчилась (I thought about how the game had ended). There are also certain myths or half-truths of traditional grammars which the present work does not seek to perpetuate, e.g., that the direct object of a negated verb must always be in the genitive, or that a negative imperative must always be imperfective. Related to this is the continual problem of textbook description of language as compared to the way it is actually used. This book points out some of the common instances in which Russian colloquial usage in particular differs from traditional textbook examples.

Suggestions for Use

The proper time to use this book is after the student has taken his first pass through the grammar with one of the many introductory textbooks. Normally this means the second year, although not necessarily the beginning of the year. Many times my experience has been that it has taken a good part of the third semester to get through the last few complicated lessons of a big book. In at least one case (the two-volume Dawson-Bidwell-Humesky Modern Russian) four semesters are necessary, moving the present review grammar ahead to the third year. It is assumed that this work will be used in conjunction with a basic-to-intermediate reader and other materials intended for composition and conversation, which could mean one to two days a week. The instructor is not advised to spend classroom time in going over the grammar presentations. Already having been exposed to most of the grammar, the student should be able to understand these succinct reviews on his own. Particular questions and problems, of course, might well be aired in class at any time.

The organization of the book is fairly simple and self-evident, as the listing of contents indicates. In general, everything pertaining to one grammatical category is found in one section, as it is in descriptive grammars, and not spread out over different lessons as it tends to be in beginning textbooks. There is no particular compulsion for the instructor to follow the sections in order. He may choose, for example, to skip the sections on phonology (3-8) or morphology (9-21) for the time being and proceed directly to those on the usage of cases (22-27). He may assign whatever he considers most necessary for his students at any given time. The arrangement of the grammatical categories, especially in sections 22 to 54, is such that there is an overall tendency for the material to increase in difficulty, although this upward curve is by no means as sharp as it is in most introductory grammars.

The exercises are intended only for practice in the mastery of grammatical principles, and not to serve as models for composition or conversation. To aid this purpose, and to prevent things from becoming merely a matter of rote, they are calculated to keep the student "on his toes." The expected will not always occur automatically; there may be an item to which the grammatical principles elucidated in that section do not apply. For example, in a conjugation exercise including искать, колебать, летать, писать, and плакать, a "regular" Conjugation I vocalic-stem verb (летать) is thrown into a series of consonant-stem verbs which have consonant changes in the present tense.

The oral drills, based chiefly on the principle of substitution, provide a framework for various possibilities. The student may practice them aloud or write them on his own; the instructor may go around the class with them, calling on one student at any point within a drill to take up where another has left off, accelerating the pace, skipping ahead, or going back and repeating. Most of them are highly condensed in form but yield dozens or even hundreds of variations, as in the following simple drill: "Make affirmative and negative sentences from the separate items of I and II in present, past, and future: I. я, он, Соколов, Анна, мы, девушки; II. дома, здесь, на собрании, у профессора." Six subjects times three tenses times two (affirmative and negative) times four predicates, plus two genders for я in the past gives 148 possibilities. The order of progression is of course variable: я дома, я здесь, я на собрании... or я дома, я был дома, я буду дома... or я дома, меня нет дома, я был дома, меня не было дома..., are just a few possibilities out of many.

Drills of the fill-in-the-blank or correct-ending type appear in many sections; the Russian may be read aloud and then translated. Straight Russian-to-English translation exercises have not been included because it is assumed the student will be doing such translation in his other reading; moreover, this type of exercise is among the easiest, since it demands only a passive knowledge of Russian (except, of course, for the time-consuming activity of looking up words in a glossary or dictionary).

The most rigorous--and in the opinion of this instructor ultimately the best--exercise is translation from English to Russian, as it demands an active knowledge of everything having to do with grammar and vocabulary. The majority of sentences in each section are based on the grammatical principles of that section and should be translated successfully by the student after some careful thought. However, certain sentences, especially in the later sections, may seem insurmountably difficult and may in fact involve constructions which have not been made

explicit in the immediately preceding discussions. And
this would naturally lead to a certain confusion. But
rather than seeming deliberately unfair, or defeating the
purpose for which this work is intended--to reinforce what
a student should already know instead of attempting to add
greatly to that knowledge--such sentences should challenge
him, forcing him to stretch his present knowledge a bit
even at the risk of giving a less than perfect answer.
Perhaps in a few cases the instructor will have to be
relied on to provide a correct translation. But one learns
by doing, and the student is more likely to have the right
way impressed on him if he has seriously tried and not completely succeeded than if he has made no attempt.

It is recommended that these translations be prepared
as homework and presented in the classroom rather than
simply handed in for the instructor to correct. The instructor might have several students give their translations of a sentence before specifying his own version,
and, although it can be time-consuming, the use of the
blackboard would be very good here: in this way the differing expressions can most easily be compared and commente
upon by others in the classroom.

In addition to the regular exercises of each section
there are supplementary translation exercises which appear
at intervals and recapitulate much of the material of the
preceding several sections.

In regard to the vocabulary of these translation exercises, I have in general tried not to require words the
second-year student would not be expected to know. In
certain cases a familiar word close in meaning can be
substituted (e.g., "I know" for "I am acquainted with";
"I think" for "I suppose"). Every now and then fancier-
than-necessary English is used deliberately to give the
student extra practice in thinking of simpler alternative
translations. Where the use of an unfamiliar Russian word
is more or less unavoidable, the Russian is given to save
the student the time and trouble of looking it up.

It is admitted that in the reality of things the
student is going to have to look up words anyway, words he
is assumed to know but has either forgotten or has never
been exposed to in the first place. An adequate dictionary
is necessary when the glossary of his first-year book fails
him, and in any case the serious student of Russian should
own a dictionary by his second year. If he has to econom-
ize, two Dover paperback republications are recommended:
M. A. O'Brien, Russian-English and English-Russian Dictionary, and A Phrase and Sentence Dictionary of Spoken Russian
(also Russian-English and English-Russian). These are
still highly serviceable books in that they give declensional and conjugational forms with stresses, and the
latter, especially, is helpful in indicating usage in
context. Most other available dictionaries, even the
more expensive ones, do not do either.

Acknowledgments

I am indebted to many individuals for reviews of
this work, with their many valuable comments, suggestions,
and corrections ranging from the most general to the most
specific. I owe particular thanks to Professors Lawrence
L. Thomas, J. Thomas Shaw, and James Bailey of the University of Wisconsin--Madison, and Professor Rasio Dunatov
of the University of Illinois at Urbana-Champaign. Professor Elena Mahlow, Mrs. Lydia M. Berkoff, and Professor
Katherina Filips-Juswigg of the University of Wisconsin--
Milwaukee were helpful in checking and correcting the
Russian examples and exercises as well as offering suggestions for revision. Far from the least of my debts is
to my colleagues who have been willing to use the grammar
and have offered valuable criticism, as well as to the
many students over the years whose experiences with the
work in its various stages have helped me in refining,
adding, or winnowing where necessary.

Although this work has been tested in many ways over
a period of several years in various classroom situations,
perfection can hardly be achieved here. Nor does the
author entertain any hopes that everyone will be satisfied.
As a first published edition, the book is bound to have
some rough edges, inconsistencies, and mistakes. Therefore, comments, corrections, and suggestions for revision,
addition, or deletion are not only invited but solicited
by the author.

Roger W. Phillips
University of Wisconsin--Milwaukee
December, 1973

CONTENTS

A Concise Russian Review Grammar

[Handwriting chart: Russian cursive alphabet, uppercase and lowercase]

А. In lower case script the only "tall" letters are б, в, and the alternative form д (not к, ъ, ы, л). Do not substitute the English ƛ for Russian к.

В. Hooks are required before л, м, я. When these occur after б, в, о, ъ, ь, з, ю, the script is broken: *Павлом*

С. Note that ж, х, з are connected from above to the preceding letter.

D. The letter х is conveniently written with two tangent semicircles instead of going back to cross it. Note how ш differs from English w.

Е. The bar below ш and above т (and sometimes н) need be used only in the case of carelessly or hastily written script.

Exercises. Write the following: 1. клюква 2. языческим 3. боязнь 4. неэкономный 5. фамилия 6. сохранивший 7. пишите 8. щегольство 9. поджёг 10. разъясниться 11. Эта живая мышь съедала всю пищу французских богачей.

2. THE SPELLING RULES

А. Rule 1: After г, к, х (called "velars") and ж, ч, ш, щ, ц (called "sibilants"), а and у are written instead of я and ю. This affects Conjugation II verbs whose stems end in ж, ч, ш, щ, as well as other verbs with consonant mutations, in the first person singular and third person plural, e.g. держу, держат from держать; кончу, кончат from кончить; пишу, пишут from писать; nouns in -жь, -чь, -шь, -щь in dative, instrumental and prepositional plural, e.g. ночам, вещами.

В. Rule 2: After these same velars and sibilants (except ц) и is written instead of ы. This affects the nominative plural of masculine nouns, e.g., ножи, языки; the genitive singular and nominative plural of feminine nouns, e.g., студентки, Маши, удачи; the masculine nominative and masculine-neuter instrumental singular and the entire

entire plural of "mixed" type adjectives, e.g., жа́ркий, жа́рким, жа́ркие. (Review the declension of adjectives in the Appendix.)

C. Rule 3: After the sibilants, an <u>unstressed</u> o is written e. This affects the genitive plural of masculine nouns in -ц, e.g., за́йцев, ме́сяцев; the instrumental singular of certain masculine and feminine nouns, e.g. това́рищем, ка́шей; the genitive, dative and prepositional singular of "mixed" adjectives in ж, ч, ш, щ, e.g., хоро́шего, хоро́шему, хоро́шем. (But note, when endings are <u>stressed</u>: отцо́в, лапшо́й, большо́й etc.)

<u>Exercises.</u> Write the correct forms of the words in parentheses. For verbs, use only the present or future perfective. 1. Учи́тель сказа́л, что э́ти (де́вушка) (хоро́шая учени́ца). 2. Они́ (положи́ть) э́ти (кни́га) и (каранда́ш) в те (я́щик). 3. Цвет (хоро́ший) апельси́на похо́ж на цвет (со́лнце) 4. Рома́н "(Оте́ц) и де́ти" знамени́тое (ру́сский) произведе́ние. 5. Ско́лько (ка́ша) вам ну́жно? 6. Я (спеши́ть) в кино́ с (това́рищ). 7. Он всегда́ пи́шет "(Дорого́й) Ива́н и Пётр", но не "(Дорого́й) Ма́ша." 8. Са́ша--учи́тель (ру́сский язы́к), а я-- учи́тель (матема́тика). 9. За (на́ша учи́тельница) стои́т две (доска́). 10. Я (держа́ть) стака́н (горя́чий) воды́ обе́ими рука́ми. 11. Па́вел рабо́тает в (большо́й), бе́лом зда́нии. 12. Пять (ме́сяц) тому́ наза́д она́ потеря́ла свой (ключ) где́- то о́коло э́той (гости́ница). 13. Ма́ша ду́мает то́лько о серь- ёзных (вещь), а не о (пустяки́). 14. Они́ (получи́ть) тряпьё от (стару́ха). 15. Мы с (Ми́ша) провели́ кани́кулы у (ба́бушка) 16. Они́ пло́хо (слу́шать) на́ши (расска́з), хотя́ они́ хорошо́ (слы́шать). 17. Ива́н пошёл за (све́жий) молоко́м для (актри́са) 18. Вы сейча́с пи́шете (каранда́ш) и́ли (ру́чка)? --Совсе́м не пишу́, у меня́ нет (бума́га). 19. Да́йте э́тим (большо́й) ма́ль- чикам (большо́й) кра́сные (я́блоко). 20. (Молодо́й пожа́рник) говоря́т по-англи́йски с тури́стам (америка́нец).

3. HARD AND SOFT CONSONANTS

A. The differences between hard and soft Russian conson- ants are most obvious in the <u>dental</u> group, which includes т, д, с, з, н, л, and р. When the soft or "palatalized" varieties of these are pronounced, with raised tongue (i.e., with more of the tongue flattened against the roof of the mouth) it can be imagined that the initial "y" element of a following е, ю or я (the letter и, although it indicates a preceding soft consonant, does not have this initial element) is so thoroughly absorbed into the consonant that it does not remain as a separate sound but alters the sound of the consonant. Note, however, that when a soft sign appears between consonant and vowel the latter retains the initial "y" sound: compare лёд (l'ot, "ice") with льёт (l'yot, "pours").

B. Perhaps the <u>hard and soft л</u> are most strikingly different to our ears, although we have something of the same contrast in English and are largely unaware of it because it does not differentiate meaning as it can in Russian (e.g., стал, "became"; сталь, "steel"). Our final "l" as in "full" approaches the Russian hard л, while the initial "l" as in "light" is more like the soft л. In English, unlike Russian, the hard sound cannot appear initially and the soft cannot appear finally.

<u>Exercises</u>. Practice the following hard and soft syllables: та/тя, тэ/те, ты/ти, то/тё, ту/тю. Repeat for д, с, з, н, л, р. Be sure to practice the trill of р, especially in the hard variety. In the soft it is lighter and less noticeable. For non-dental consonants: practice the same contrasts with the <u>labials</u> п, б, в and м, and for the <u>velars</u> к, г, х, in which pairing is virtually non-existent, use only ка, ке, ки, ко, ку, etc. Then proceed to the words and sentences below:

1. тя́нут, тётя, писа́тель, мать, говори́ть 2. де́лать, дя́дя, бу́дет, иди́те, судьба́ 3. ся́ду, сюда́, всё, письмо́, здесь 4. зима́, взять, возьму́ 5. нет, ня́ня, день 6. ла́мпа, ми́лый, в углу́, стол, столь 7. ля́мка, люблю́, нельзя́, то́лько, сталь, ста́ли 8. ряд, ры́ба, гроб, инжене́р 9. ряд, река́, грёб, тепе́рь, говорю́

10. И тётя и мать хотя́т говори́ть о писа́телях. 11. Дя́дя бу́дет держа́ть за́ руку Ди́му, когда́ пойдёт на сва́дьбу. 12. Сего́дня Са́ша ся́дет сюда́ и напи́шет все пи́сьма. 13. Нельзя́ вози́ть зе́лень зимо́й; я сам возьму́. 14. Сего́дня ня́ня Ма́шенька ню́нит: у неё нет де́нег. 15. Ну ла́дно, ми́лый, поло́жим ла́мпу на по́лку в углу́ ло́дки. 16. То́лько лихи́е лю́ди гуля́ли по льду́ без шля́пы. 17. Бра́тья инжене́ры бы́ли ра́ды лови́ть ры́бу за́ городом. 18. Тепе́рь я говорю́ о ря́де интере́сных рек.

4. VOICED AND VOICELESS CONSONANTS

There are six pairs of such consonants: the voiced б, в, г, д, ж, з and their respective voiceless equivalents п, ф, к, т, ш, с. In addition there are the unpaired voiceless consonants х, ц, ч, and щ.

A. <u>Voiced consonants</u> are normally pronounced like their voiceless equivalents (1) at the end of a word, except before words closely connected with it such as particles and the past tense of "to be"; (2) before a voiceless consonant in the middle of a word (here г > х before к or ч).

4

B. Voiceless consonants become voiced before a voiced consonant, except before в, (1) in the middle of a word; (2) in certain cases at the end of a word before the past tense of "to be" and particles beginning with a voiced consonant.

Note that these assimilations include the final consonants of prepositions and certain adverbs which are pronounced together with the following word. A common and fairly serious mistake of the elementary student is to pronounce a prepositional phrase like в парке as "vuh parke" rather than the correct "fparke". It is better not to hear a preposition like в at all than to have it pronounced separately from the following word.

Exercises. Practice pronouncing the following words and sentences: 1. хлеб, столб, любовь, друг, пирог, обед, город, тетрадь, гараж, глаз, сквозь 2. всё, входит, в кино, в поле, из сада, общий, бегство, двадцать, водка, мягкий, под снегом, ложка, дождь, поезд 3. также, как дела, как бы, вокзал, к жене, к дому, к городу, с горы, сделать, с запада, свой, просьба, отзыв, от брата, от города, отдал, может быть, отец был, успех же 4. Глеб и Любовь шли в кино под дождём. 5. Вообще, легче пить водку из стакана. 6. Как дела на вокзале? 7. Может быть, пакет был от брата. 8. Мы сделаем ножки для стола. 9. Куда мне идти? к другу или к жене? 10. Он совсем не знает своей жены.

5. DIFFICULT CONSONANTS AND CONSONANT CLUSTERS

A. A common mistake is to pronounce Russian х too much like English "k", when it is much closer to "h", being similar to the slight fricative sound heard in "huge."

B. The consonants ж , ц and ш are always hard, regardless of whether they are followed by е, и, or ь. This is especially noticeable when a following и is pronounced as ы.

C. The consonants ч and щ are always soft, regardless of a following а, о or у. Ч is pronounced like "sh" before т in что and its compounds and before н in a few words, among them конечно and скучно. There are two pronunciations of щ: "sh-ch" as in "fresh cheese," and a long soft "sh" as in "fresh sheets."

D. The fricatives с and з combine with ш, ж and ч in the following ways: сш, зш = long ш; сж, зж = long ж; сч, зч = щ.

E. In clusters of three dental consonants one is dropped in pronunciation: д in здн, т in стн, стл, л in солнце. Also note the drop of the first в in вств.

F. There are many consonant clusters which do not appear
in English. See Exercise 10 below.

Exercises. Practice the following: 1. хорошо́, хи́мия,
хохо́чет, успе́х, заво́дах, прохо́д, ша́хматы, лёгкий 2. центр,
конце́рт, ци́фра, об отце́, маши́на, жить 3. часы́, по́чта,
чтобы, щу́ка, борщ, защи́та 4. с ша́ром, из ша́ра, с жено́й,
сейча́с же, из жа́лости, сча́стье 5. Во хмелю́, хра́брый архи́п
хорошо́ хохо́чет о свои́х лёгких успе́хах в колхо́зах. 6. В
це́нтре Цинцинна́ти, в це́ркви и в ци́рке, мы це́лый ме́сяц ду́-
мали об отце́. 7. Чтобы хорошо́ служи́ть секрета́ршей, коне́ч-
но нужна́ пи́шущая маши́нка. 8. Расска́зчик счита́л, что
Зо́щенко успе́шно защища́л отста́ющего това́рища. 9. Че́стное
сло́во, все на со́лнце чу́вствуют себя́ счастли́выми в пра́здник.
10. вбежа́ть, вдоль, взять, взгляд, взро́слый, вкус, власть,
вме́сто, внеза́пно, вперёд, врач, всегда́, встре́тить, второ́й,
входи́ть, вчера́, гва́рдия, где, гнев, дверь, дли́нный, Дми́трий
дневни́к, жгут, ждёт, жмёт, жнёт, жре́бий, звезда́, зда́ние,
здра́вствуйте, зло, змея́, зна́ет, зре́ние, кварти́ра, кни́га,
кста́ти, кто, льда, лгать, мгнове́ние, мла́дший, мно́го, мра́ч-
ный, мще́ние, нра́вится, пти́ца, пчела́, рвать, рта, сбо́рник,
свет, сде́лать, срок, схе́ма, сце́на, твой, тле́ние, тьма,
хвост, хлеб, хму́рый, цвет, член, чрезвыча́йно, что, шля́па

6. VOWEL QUALITY AND REDUCTION

A. The most difficult of the vowels for the non-Slavic
student to pronounce is ы. It is deeper, more guttural
than the vowel in English "bill." One way to aim at it
is to spread the lips for "ee" and try to say "oo". A
common mistake is to pronounce it with an initial "oo" or
"w" sound, then move to "ee", making a diphthong out of
it (as in the often heard "vwee" for вы).

B. Another common mistake is to pronounce stressed о like
the English "oh" as in "show," which is in reality a diphthong, rounded to "oo" at the end. Care should be taken
to pronounce this vowel more like the "aw" in "Shaw."

C. Stressed e before a soft consonant is "raised" in an-
ticipation of the following palatalized sound; that is,
it becomes like the "long a" in "bait" (without, however,
approaching the diphthongal "ay") as opposed to the "short
e" in "bet," heard before hard consonants or at the end
of a word.

D. The vowels ы/и and у/ю undergo no appreciable reduction
but maintain their basic quality in any syllable, with the
reservation that unstressed и is more like the "short i"
of "bit" than the "ee" of "beet." In the syllable just
before the stressed one ("first pretonic") and the initial
position if unstressed, а and о reduce to a vowel like the

"short u" of "but"; in all other unstressed syllables they
reduce entirely to э, the indistinct, neutral sound heard
at the end of "sofa." In all pretonic syllables, е and я
are pronounced like unstressed и, while after the stressed
syllable ("posttonic") the two are somewhat differentiated:
е normally retains its pretonic value but я is further re-
duced to э. It should be noted that in <u>foreign-derived</u>
<u>words</u> the tendency is for о and е(э) to retain their
stressed values in unstressed syllables.

E. The peculiarities of Russian spelling obscure certain
values. The combinations жи, ши, ци and unstressed же,
ше, це must be pronounced as жы, шы, цы, since these
consonants are always hard. Pretonic ча and ща are really
like чя and щя since these consonants are always soft, and
are therefore to be pronounced as unstressed чи, щи.

<u>Exercises</u>. Practice the following: 1. ты, вы, быть, был,
была, были, столы 2. это, еду, газета, ответ, смотрел,
все, эти, едет, о газете, ответь, смотрели, всеми
3. хорошо, болото, золото, меня, тебя, язык, пятидесятом,
облаков, автомобиль, радио, поэт, энергия 4. часы, щадить,
жена, жизнь, шептать, целебный 5. Мы смотрим в окно на
балкон Набокова: вот он ходит и пьёт вино. 6. Мы с сыном
были на выставке, где кто-то положил цветы на все столы.
7. Целый день, они сидели за этими газетами на столе; они
осмотрели все объявления. 8. Кто-то говорит по радио, что
озеро около болота, которое хорошо отражало молочное об-
лако, околдовало поэта. 9. Теперь у меня энергичная
пятидесятилетняя жена: она не щадит себя, но часами я
должен терпеть её тяжёлый язык.

7. WORD STRESS

A. In Russian there is no secondary stress, as in English
or German, but only <u>one</u> stress per word, no matter how
long. The next strongest syllable in a Russian word is
the first pretonic, which in English happens to be the
weakest. Compare "administration" with администрация.
In Russian there is a steady rise to the stressed syllable
while in English it is more "up and down."

B. A kind of secondary stress may occur in compound words
or numerals such as тёмно-красный, железоделательный,
пятидесятилетие. But it is usually the case that, even
though the vowel of the first part of the compound may
retain its stressed value, there is only one actual stress.

C. The single stress includes also monosyllabic prepositions and particles associated with the word, so that they
are pronounced together as if they were part of the word:
от брата as одбрата, не знает as низнает, читал бы as

читáлбы, etc. However, sometimes the preposition or the particles не, ни take the stress, in which case the following word loses its normal stress. Common examples: зá город, зá руку, нá пол, пó полу, пó полю, нé было, нé дал

<u>Exercises</u>. Practice the following stresses: 1. зáработок, дéятельность, образовáние, кровотечéние, обрáзованный, сельскохозя́йственное, достопримечáтельности, проводники́, карандашá 2. гóрсовéт, грóмкоговори́тель, трёхнедéльный, 3. под сту́лом, на доскé, по мостовóй, не дéлают, я хотéл бы, ни жив ни мёртв, о чём-то, кáк-нибудь, Тáня же 4. Во втóрник Ивáн не рабóтал на завóде от пяти́ до семи́, но ходи́л по мостовóй со свои́м дру́гом и говори́л о поэ́зии. 5. Для пикникá зá городом нé было стакáнов, потому́ что Сáша нé дал их нам но брóсил их нá пол. 6. Вáня же никогдá нé жил там. 7. Я хотéл бы знать чтó-нибудь.

8. SENTENCE INTONATION

A. The most typical Russian intonation is downward or <u>falling</u>, as opposed to the English, which is most often rising. Because of this difference, which holds for neutral statements, exclamations, commands and questions with interrogative words, it may seem to us that the speaker is bored, impatient or being peremptory, which is not necessarily the case. The emphasized word (carrying the sentence stress, underlined in the above patterns) is most often final and spoken with a drop in pitch together with the rise in volume.

B. With an interrogative word in a question, the voice is dropped at the end as it is for statements, but without such a word, the voice must <u>rise</u> to indicate that it is a question, as in English.

C. If the emphasized word is in the middle of the sentence, the intonation is <u>rising-falling</u>. Note that when the emphasis is initial or medial rather than final, the drop in pitch is more precipitous.

Exercises. Read the illustrative patterns above, and practice also the following intonations: 1. Закройте, пожалуйста, <u>дверь</u>. 2. Сколько у вас <u>детей</u>? 3. Сколько у <u>вас</u> детей? 4. Что вы <u>знаете</u>? 5. <u>Что</u> вы знаете? 6. А что <u>вы</u> знаете? 7. Алекса́ша здесь? 8. Да, Алекса́ша здесь. 9. Нет, Алекса́ши нет здесь. 10. Мы никогда́ не́ жили <u>там</u>. 11. Мы <u>никогда</u> не́ жили там.

9. GENDER

Gender in Russian is fairly simple: nouns ending in a consonant (including й) not followed by ь are <u>masculine</u>; those in a or я <u>feminine</u>; those in o or e(ё) <u>neuter</u>. But there are a couple of situations in which the gender of a noun is not readily apparent from its ending:

A. <u>Nouns in -ь</u>. The majority, including all those having the suffix -ость and those in sibilants (-жь, -чь, -шь, -щь) are <u>feminine</u>: дверь, но́вость, вещь, ночь, etc. The following groups are <u>masculine</u>: (1) nouns denoting <u>male</u> beings, especially those in -тель (of which the feminine is -тельница): писа́тель, writer; учи́тель, teacher; вождь, leader; гость, guest (fem. го́стья); князь, prince; коро́ль, king; царь, tsar; секрета́рь, secretary (fem. секрета́рша) (2) names of certain <u>animals</u>: го́лубь, pigeon, dove; гусь, goose; зверь, beast; конь, cavalry horse; медве́дь, bear (but ло́шадь, horse, and мышь, mouse, are feminine); (3) names of <u>months</u>: янва́рь, февра́ль, etc. Other common masculine nouns include: автомоби́ль, automobile; гвоздь, nail; день,* day; дождь, rain; ка́мень,* stone; ко́рень,* root; кора́бль, ship; ло́коть,* elbow; но́готь,* nail (on finger or toe); ого́нь,* fire; пень,* stub, stump; путь, way, voyage (irregularly declined, see 16A); роя́ль, (grand) piano; рубль, ruble; слова́рь, dictionary, vocabulary; спекта́кль, show; стиль, style; у́голь,* coal; у́ровень,* degree, level; фона́рь, lantern, light. The nouns marked with an asterisk have a "mobile vowel"; see 14A.

B. <u>Masculine Nouns in -a/-я</u>. These include (1) nouns denoting <u>male</u> persons: мужчи́на, man, male; ю́ноша, youth; дя́дя, uncle; де́душка, grandfather; судья́, judge; слуга́, servant; (2) certain masculine <u>names</u> and <u>all</u> <u>diminutives</u> of Russian masculine names: Илья́, Elijah; Фома́, Thomas; Ва́ня, Johnny; Ми́ша, Mike. Although these are declined like feminine nouns, all adjectives and pronouns modifying them, as well as verbs in the past tense, must be masculine: большо́й мужчи́на, ваш дя́дя, де́душка был, etc.

C. For the gender of <u>indeclinable foreign borrowings</u>, see 11B.

Exercises. (a) General oral and/or written drill on gender and declension. Review the regular declensions of nouns and adjectives in the Appendix. Combine each item of I

and III in singular and plural (total possible sentences:
420): I. это, я смотрю на, иду к, иду от, сижу за, думаю о
II. интере́сный, ру́сский, хоро́ший, большо́й, после́дний
III. ма́льчик, автомоби́ль, кресло́, зда́ние, маши́на, ста́нция,
    дверь
(b) Supply the correct forms of the words in parentheses:
1. (Large) кора́бль приста́л к бе́регу и лю́ди подошли́ к (кре́-
пость). 2. У нас 21-го ию́ня (long) день и (short) ночь.
3. (Your) де́душка не смог найти́ э́того сло́ва в (слова́рь).
4. Лю́ба (worked) всё у́тро в по́ле, а Ко́ля (sat) до́ма. 5. Я
зна́ю то́лько (one good) же́нщину и (one good) мужчи́ну. 6. На
дворе́ мы уви́дели (ло́шадь) и (медве́дь). 7. (This) писа́тель
иногда́ говори́т с (коро́ль). 8. У нас быва́ет о́тпуск то́лько
в (May) и в (September). 9. (Old) ба́бушка до́лго говори́ла
с (young) судьёй. 10. Секрета́рь (came) из конто́ры и (saw
Mike). 11. "Мы до́лго стоя́ли под (strong rain) и смотре́л на
(я́ркий) фона́рь у (door) большо́го до́ма," (said the old) слуга́

10. ANIMATE NOUNS

A. **The animate category** applies to nouns denoting living
beings, including animals as low on the scale as insects
but not plants, and their modifiers. This animateness is
retained when they are used in inanimate contexts such as
titles, e.g., чита́ть "Идио́та", to read <u>The Idiot</u>, or names
of things, e.g., бро́сить короля́, discard a king (in cards).
In this category also note мертве́ц, corpse. On the other
hand, collective nouns such as наро́д, the people, and
то́лпы, crowds, referring to groups of animate beings, are
considered inanimate: он хорошо́ зна́ет ру́сский наро́д, he
knows the Russian people well.

B. <u>Gender and Declension</u>. For <u>masculine</u> nouns, both the
accusative singular and plural take the genitive forms:
мы уви́дели краси́вого орла́, we saw a beautiful eagle; мы
уви́дели краси́вых орло́в, we saw the beautiful eagles. For
<u>feminine</u> nouns, only the accusative plural is involved
since they have the special form -у (ю) in the singular--
except for those in -ь; note: я встре́тил дочь, I met the
daughter; я встре́тил дочере́й, I met the daughters. The
few <u>neuter</u> nouns considered animate show a difference between the singular, in which the accusative is like the
nominative, and the plural, in which it takes the form of
the genitive. Except for an archaic noun or two, these
are adjectival forms which refer to animals, among them
живо́тное, animal, and насеко́мое, insect. Compare они́
нашли́ живо́тное, they found an animal, with они́ нашли́
живо́тных, they found the animals.

<u>Exercises</u>. Translate: 1. In the park the doctor sat down
on a bronze horse (ме́дный конь) and watched birds. 2. He
also likes to watch interesting insects. 3. Come here and

see this beautiful insect! 4. Can you recall the wives
of Henry (Ге́нрих) VIII? 5. No, I can recall only one
wife--my own. 6. They said about Swift that he loved
mankind but not people. 7. When I look at my horse (use
ло́шадь), I remember that Jack hated horses. 8. I like
the American people, but I don't like crowds. 9. What
Russian novels are you reading? 10. Well, let's see--
this semester we are reading <u>Eugene (Евге́ний) Onegin</u>, <u>A
Hero of Our Time</u>, <u>Dead Souls</u>, <u>Oblomov</u>, and <u>Fathers and
Children</u>. 11. Next semester we will read <u>Mother</u>, <u>The
Petty Demon</u> (Ме́лкий бес), <u>Cities and Years</u>, <u>The Embezzlers</u>
(Растра́тчики) and <u>The Quiet Don</u>. 12. And after that,
maybe I'll want to read Ogden Nash.

11. NOUNS USED ONLY IN PLURAL; INDECLINABLE NOUNS

A. <u>Common Nouns Used Only in Plural</u> include (with the genitive given in parentheses): брю́ки (брюк), trousers;
воро́та (воро́т), gate; де́ньги (де́нег), money; дрова́ (дров),
firewood; кани́кулы (кани́кул), summer vacation; но́жницы
(но́жниц), scissors; обо́и (обо́ев), wallpaper; очки́ (очко́в),
glasses; по́хороны (похоро́н), funeral; са́ни (сане́й),
sleigh; сли́вки (сли́вок), cream; черни́ла (черни́л), ink;
ша́хматы (ша́хмат), chess; штаны́ (штано́в), pants; щи (щей),
cabbage soup. These nouns have no singular forms and con-
sequently must be used with <u>plural</u> modifiers, even when
the meaning is obviously singular. In the case of numerals, they are used with одни́ and the collectives дво́е,
тро́е, че́тверо and the genitive plural, rather than the
cardinals два, три, четы́ре, which can take only the genitive singular. Also belonging to this group, of course,
is часы́ (часо́в) in the meaning of "clock, watch."

B. <u>Indeclinable Nouns</u>. All foreign borrowings ending in
-е(э), -и, -о, and -у(ю) are indeclinable, as well as
names of women (but not men) ending in a consonant, certain nouns and all names ending in stressed -а́. Some of
the most commonly used are: бюро́, office; кино́, cinema,
movie theater; ко́фе, coffee; мада́м, madame; меню́, menu;
метро́, subway; пальто́, overcoat; ра́дио, radio; такси́,
taxi; шоссе́, highway. The inanimate nouns are <u>neuter</u>,
except for ко́фе, which is masculine. Although these nouns
never change in form, their modifiers must be declined
according to gender, number and case, and verbs must agree
in number and gender.

<u>Exercises</u>. Translate: 1. I have two watches and three
radios. 2. Does Sasha like hot coffee? 3. He wrote with
red ink. 4. Cabbage soup was on the menu. 5. The gate
opens and the sleigh enters. 6. The gates open and the
sleighs enter. 7. Give Susan Peterson your overcoats and
Henry Peterson your pants. 8. Have you read Flaubert?
No, but I have read Dumas and Zola. 9. He was standing
between the big white taxis. 10. Our vacation began in
New York and ended at Pedro's funeral in Chicago.

A. "Locative" Singular. Certain inanimate masculine nouns, mostly monosyllabic, take stressed -ý(ю́) after the prepositions в and на, while retaining the regular -е after other prepositions. Some of the more common are: бал, (social) ball; бéрег, bank, shore; бой, battle; вéтер, wind; глаз, eye; год, year; гроб, coffin; дым, smoke; край, edge, region; круг, circle; лёд, ice; лес, forest; лоб, forehead; мост, bridge; нос, nose; плен, captivity; пол, floor; пот, sweat; пруд, pond; рай, heaven, paradise; рот, mouth; ряд, row; сад, garden; снег, snow; угол, corner; шкаф, cupboard. Some of these have a "mobile vowel" (see 14A): на ветрý, на лбу, на льду, во рту, в углý.

B. "Partitive" Singular. A very few masculine nouns of a collective nature may take the ending -у(ю) in place of the regular -а(я) in a partitive sense ("part, some of") after nouns, adverbs or verbs indicating quantity. The two most commonly used this way are чай, tea, and сáхар, sugar. With a modifier, however, the regular ending is used: я хочý чáю, I want some tea; but я хочý хорóшего чáя, I want some good tea. Also note the expressions мнóго нарóду, a lot of people, as a colloquial equivalent of мнóго людéй, and из дому, away from home (cf. из дóма, out of the house.)

Exercises. (a) Oral drill: combine the verbs, wherever appropriate, with the prepositional expressions: I. Мы рабóтаем, игрáем, идём, сидим в (на) II. бéрег, двор, круг, лёд, лес, мост, пол, рай, ресторáн, ряд, сад, снег, ýгол, ýлица
(b) Supply the correct forms: 1. Онá налилá мне чáшку (tea) 2. Это случилось в 1949-ом (year). 3. Я купил (some tea and sugar) в магазине на том (corner). 4. Мы вышли (out of the house) и вошли в (woods) 5. Сáша убежáл (away from home) и скрывáлся всю ночь в (forest). 6. Дáйте мне, пожáлуйста, кусóк (sugar). 7. (Many people) спросило егó, что у негó на (nose). 8. Мáша упáла на (ice) и оказáлась на (edge) большóй прóруби. 9. Хóчешь крéпкого или жидкого (tea)? 10. Пáвел сидéл на (floor) и писáл о своём (garden) 11. Мне совсéм не нрáвится цвет (of the tea). 12. Сегóдня мнóго лóдок на (shore).

13. THE GENITIVE PLURAL OF NOUNS

A. The most typical ending for the genitive plural is the "zero", expressed by: (1) nothing, in hard feminine nouns in -a and neuter nouns in -о, e.g., кóмната/кóмнат, дéло/ дел. In addition, certain masculine nouns have no ending; among the most common are глаз, eye; раз, time; солдáт, soldier; and человéк, man, person (used only after numbers); (2) -ь for soft feminine nouns in -я preceded by a

consonant, e.g., неде́ля/неде́ль (for exceptions, see 14B);
(3) -й for neuter nouns in -ие and feminine nouns in -ия,
e.g., зда́ние/зда́ний, а́рмия/а́рмий

B. The ending -ов is used for masculine nouns ending in a
consonant other than ж, ч, ш, щ, e.g., стол/столо́в. The
soft variant -ев (-ёв, stressed) is for nouns in -й or -ц
(when the ending is unstressed; -цо́в when stressed), e.g.,
музе́й/музе́ев, бой/боёв, ме́сяц/ме́сяцев. In addition,
о́блако, cloud, has облако́в; пла́тье, dress, has пла́тьев.

C. The ending -ей is used for all nouns in -ь, masculine
nouns in the sibilants ж, ч, ш, щ, and feminine nouns in
stressed -ья́, e.g., гость/госте́й, дверь/двере́й, нож/
ноже́й, свинья́/свине́й. Also note that ружьё, gun; мо́ре,
sea; по́ле, field; дя́дя, uncle; ю́ноша, youth, take this
ending.

Exercises. Supply the correct forms: 1. Невозмо́жно вести́
иссле́дования без (laboratories). 2. У нас мно́го (doors),
но нет (keys). 3. В э́том кварта́ле живёт то́лько 5 (семья́),
и ме́жду ни́ми 12 (автомоби́ль). 4. Орёл лете́л вы́ше (than
the clouds). 5. В тума́не мо́жно бы́ло ви́деть не́сколько
(streets) и (buildings). 6. Мы уви́дели (soldiers) и за-
интересова́лись цве́том их (костю́мы). 7. За обе́дом я всегда́
ем мно́го (хлеб), а (молоко́) пью ма́ло. 8. На́ши кани́кули
пролете́ли бы́стро и без (собы́тия). 9. В э́той ча́сти све́та
мно́го (пусты́ня) и ма́ло (лес). 10. Со́ня посмотре́ла на
(those geniuses) и спроси́ла, почему́ у них нет краси́вых
(eyes). 11. Его́ го́лос дошёл до нас с (mountains). 12. На
э́той неде́ле Степа́н позвони́л мне три (times), а на про́шлой
неде́ле шесть (times). 13. Я встре́тил (your uncles), когда́
речь шла о цене́ (of dresses). 14. Я не понима́ю ни (ideas)
э́тих (францу́з) ни (тео́рии) э́тих (не́мец). 15. Ско́лько
(газе́та) выхо́дит в э́том го́роде, и ско́лько (статья́) в них?

14. THE MOBILE VOWEL

A. Masculine Nouns. The "mobile" or "fleeting" vowel о
or е appears only in the nominative singular. In the
examples below, the genitive singular is given as contrast to the nominative. Nouns in -ок and -ец regularly
lose this vowel in declension: кусо́к/куска́, оте́ц/отца́,
etc. But note that in уро́к, lesson, восто́к, east, and a
few other nouns, the о is retained because it is a part
of the root, not a suffix. In a few words such as кузне́ц,
blacksmith, and мертве́ц, corpse, the е is retained to
avoid difficult consonant clusters. After л, е is replaced by ь: па́лец/па́льца finger. If it follows a vowel,
it becomes й: бое́ц/бойца́, warrior. Other nouns include
ве́тер, wind; день, day; ка́мень, stone; ковёр, rug; ко́рень,
root; костёр, bonfire; лев, lion; лёд, ice; лоб, forehead;

ло́коть, elbow; но́готь, fingernail; ове́с, oats; ого́нь, fire; орёл, eagle; Па́вел, Paul; пень, stump; посо́л, ambassador; рот, mouth; ручёй (gen. ручья́) stream; сон, sleep, dream; у́гол, corner, angle; у́голь, coal; у́ровень, level.

B. **Feminine and Neuter Nouns.** The mobile vowel appears in the genitive plural when the ending -a(я) or o is preceded by two consonants or more, e.g., кра́ска, окно́, полоте́нце. With nouns in -ка, the inserted vowel is o (e after ж,ч,ш, Spelling Rule No. 3): таре́лка/таре́лок, но́жка/но́жек. When к is preceded by й the latter becomes e: тро́йка/тро́ек. Note that this does not happen in certain nouns in -на: война́, war; та́йна, secret. In other nouns, the vowel inserted between consonants is regularly e, except after the velars г,к,х, when o is used, e.g. кре́сло/кре́сел; окно́/о́кон. Note that when -ня is preceded by a consonant, the н in the genitive plural is **hard**, e.g., пе́сня/пе́сен, song. Exceptions: ку́хня/ку́хонь, kitchen; дере́вня/дереве́нь, village. Note the unique mobile и in яйцо́/яи́ц, egg.

Vowels are **not inserted** before dental or labial stops (д, т, б, п), or в, e.g., пра́вда/правд, по́чта/почт, изба́/изб, бога́тство/бога́тств. They are usually not inserted before р, e.g., и́скра/искр, but note ребро́/рёбер, rib; сестра́/сестёр, sister.

In a very few **feminine nouns in -ь**, a mobile o appears in the nominative/accusative and instrumental singular: ложь/лжи, ло́жью, lie; also рожь, rye; вошь, louse; любо́вь, love; це́рковь, church. (When used as a woman's name, Любо́вь retains the o throughout the declension.)

Exercises. (a) Oral drill: repeat each phrase of I with the proper form of each noun in II:
I. Мы говори́ли о; Ско́лько у вас   II. замо́к, пода́рок, песо́к, ребёнок, стари́к, иностра́нец, молоде́ц, ме́сяц, буты́лка, оши́бка, руба́шка, фа́брика, хозя́йка, ша́пка

(b) Supply the correct forms: 1. Ва́ря с (child) подошла́ к (Americans). 2. Мы все собрали́сь о́коло (bonfire), се́ли на (stumps) и на́чали петь о том, как со́лнце восхо́дит на (east) 3. Лю́ди со всех (ends) све́та прихо́дят к (father). 4. У нас на рука́х 10 (fingers) и 10 (fingernails). 5. Что э́то у вас на (forehead)? --Я упа́л на (ice). 6. Он собира́ется провести́ пять (days) у (Pavel) и́ли у (Lev). 7. Во (dream) я броса́л (stones) на (ambassador). 8. На (lesson) никто́ не услы́шал (bell). 9. Са́ша дал ло́шади три (pieces) са́хару, и она́ то́же хоте́ла (oats). 10. Мы с (blacksmith) смотре́ли на (fire) в (corner).

(c) Translate: 1. I saw the girls in church. 2. Nina found ten kopecks by the boxes in front of the church. 3. Ivan received many letters from his sisters. 4. How

many windows do these kitchens have? 5. We don't have
any cups, plates or forks. 6. I don't know the forms of
these numbers. 7. Sasha had no love for Lyubov.
8. Sonya sang several songs about love. 9. We have too
many wars; we'll never get to the stars. 10. There are
no societies without games.

15. IRREGULAR PLURALS

A. <u>Nominative Plural in -á(я́)</u>. Certain masculine nouns
take this ending, always stressed, instead of the regular
-ы(и). Common <u>inanimate nouns</u> include: áдрес, address;
бéрег, shore, bank; вéчер, evening; глаз, eye; гóлос,
voice; гóрод, city; дом, house; кóлокол, bell; край, edge,
region; лес, forest; луг, meadow; нóмер, number; óстров,
island; пóезд, train; рог, horn; рукáв, sleeve; счёт,
account, bill. Note the differentiation of meaning in
цвет/цветá, colors, and цветóк/цветы́, flowers. Animate
nouns denoting <u>profession or occupation</u> often have this
ending: дирéктор, director; дóктор, doctor; кондýктор,
conductor (on public transportation); мáстер, foreman,
master craftsman; пóвар, cook; профéссор, professor;
стóрож, guard, watchman; учи́тель, teacher.

B. <u>Nominative Plural in -ья</u>. Some masculine and neuter
nouns have -ь- plus <u>soft</u> endings throughout the plural.
The following have nom. -ья, gen.-ьев, dat. -ьям, etc:
брат, brother; стул, chair; дéрево, tree; крылó, wing;
перó, feather, pen. In the three neuter nouns, the
stress moves back one syllable from the endings in the
plural. Note the double meaning of лист in the plural:
ли́стья, leaves; листы́, sheets of paper. When the plural
endings are stressed, the genitive is in -éй rather than
-ьев: друг/друзья́, друзéй, -ья́м etc., friend; муж/мужья́,
husband; сын/сыновья́, son. Note the changes in друг and
сын, which occur throughout the plural.

C. <u>Nominative Plural in -и</u>. Neuter nouns in -ко, many of
them diminutives, take -и in the nominative plural, e.g.
окóшко, (little) window; вéко, eyelid; я́блоко, apple.
The genitive has the normal "zero" ending, but note the
exception óблако/облакá, облакóв, cloud. The following
neuter parts of the body take -и: плечó/плéчи, shoulder;
брюхо/брю́хи, belly; and with consonant change ýхо, ear:
ýши, ушéй, ушáм, etc. Note the soft plural endings
throughout of колéно, knee: колéни, колéней, колéням, etc.
The masculine noun сосéд, neighbor, has the same soft
endings in plural.

D. <u>Plural of Nouns in -ин</u>. For nouns ending in -анин
(янин) such as англичáнин, Englishman, крестья́нин, peasant,
the final ин is dropped in the plural and these endings
added: nom. -е gen. zero, dat. -ам, etc. Note also

господи́н, gentleman, Mr: господа́, господ, господа́м, etc;
хозя́ин, owner, master, host: хозя́ева, хозя́ев, etc.

E. **Plural of Nouns in -ёнок.** These nouns, denoting the
offspring of animals, take the plural endings -я́та, -я́т,
-я́там, etc., e.g. поросёнок/по[ро]ся́та, suckling pig. Note
that in the case of ребёнок, child, the plural ребя́та is
colloquial and has the meaning of "guys, fellows" as well
as "kids." Normally, "children" is де́ти (see 16B).

Exercises. Oral Drills. (1) Repeat I with each noun of
II in its proper form: I. Скажи́те мне, пожа́луйста, где
нахо́дятся э́ти II. а́дрес, го́род, де́рево, дом, заво́д, лес,
но́мер, по́езд, стол, стул, счёт, цвето́к
(2) I. У нас в э́той гости́нице живу́т II. брат, граждани́н,
дире́ктор, до́ктор, друг, инжене́р, конду́ктор, ма́стер, меха́-
ник, по́вар, профе́ссор, сто́рож, учи́тель
(b) Supply the correct forms: 1. (The professors) сиде́ли
под (trees), когда́ (leaves) па́дали на них. 2. Де́вочка
положи́ла (flowers) ме́жду (sheets of paper). 3. Ско́лько у
вас (sons)? --У меня́ два (sons). 4. Почему́ (doctors)
всегда́ пи́шут (with pens)? 5. Я ви́дел (forests and meadows)
э́той страны́, но не ви́дел (cities). 6. Мои́ (brothers) чита́-
ли вслух "(Evenings) на ху́торе близ Дика́нки". 7. Вы зна́ете
(roots) э́тих слов? --Нет, их то́лько (teachers) зна́ют.
8. Нам ну́жно пять (chairs) для ва́ших (husbands). 9. Вам
нра́вятся (colors) э́тих иску́сственных (flowers)? 10.(Trains)
ча́сто прохо́дят че́рез (these cities).

(c) Translate: 1. Peter has broad shoulders but also a
big belly. 2. He doesn't like his neighbors, and I don't
like peasants. 3. Give these apples to our guys, but not
to the Englishmen. 4. Six little pigs went to town, but
only three little pigs returned. 5. When the plane flew
into the clouds, our ears began to hurt. 6. "Gentlemen," he began, but he should have said "Citizens."
7. Kolya was standing on his knees behind one of the
little windows. 8. We heard their voices but saw only
their eyes. 9. Don't have a hundred rubles, but have a
hundred friends.

16. OTHER IRREGULAR NOUNS

A. **Nouns with Infixes in Singular and Plural.** A group of
neuter nouns ending in -мя have the infix -ен- (see the
Appendix for declension). The most common of these are:
бре́мя, burden; вре́мя, time; зна́мя, flag, banner (plural
знамёна); и́мя, name; пла́мя, flame (plural not used); се́мя,
seed (gen. pl. семя́н). Note: the masculine noun путь,
way, path, journey, has the same endings in the singular,
although stressed: gen., dat., prep. пути́, inst. путём.
But in the plural the endings remain soft: пути́, -е́й, -я́м.

The nouns мать, mother, and дочь, daughter, have -ep-
throughout the declension: singular ма́тери (gen., dat.,
prep.), ма́терью (inst.), plural ма́тери, матере́й, матеря́м,
etc. The nouns не́бо, sky, and чу́до, miracle, have the
infix -ес- in the <u>plural</u> only: небеса́, небе́с, небеса́м.

B. <u>The nouns де́ти and лю́ди</u>, plural only, are declined
thus: дете́й, де́тям, детьми́, де́тях. (The rare instrumental
plural form -ьми́ also occurs in дочь, daughter, and
ло́шадь, horse.) The archaic singular дитя́, child, has
been replaced by ребёнок, and the singular of лю́ди, people,
men, is челове́к. Note that челове́к is used as the genitive plural after numbers; however: мно́го люде́й, many
people. With де́ти, as with all nouns having only a plural
form, the collectives дво́е, тро́е, че́тверо must be used
rather than the cardinals два, три, четы́ре, which can take
only a genitive singular.

<u>Exercises</u>. (a) Oral drill. Combine the quantifiers of I,
where appropriate, with each noun of II:
I. У меня́ оди́н, два, три, пять, мно́го, нет II. вре́мя,
дочь, и́мя, ребёнок, се́мя, семья́, челове́к

(b) Supply the correct forms: 1. (Daughters) Кузнецо́ва
уже́ пришли́. Вы по́мните их (names)? 2. Так как у него́ не́
было (time) разгова́ривать да́льше с на́ми, мы пожела́ли ему́
счастли́вого (journey). 3. Со́ня (meanwhile) стоя́ла ме́жду
(horses) и моли́лась о (miracle). 4. Коро́ль разгова́ривал
с (daughter) и она́ ему́ сказа́ла, "Дай (the people) что они́
хотя́т." 5. (Mothers) взя́ли (children) в го́род, а пото́м
(children) потащи́ли (mothers) в кино́. 6. Вчера́ я встре́тила
ва́шу (mother) на у́лице. Она́ несла́ огро́мное (flag). 7.
Ско́лько у Па́влова (children)? Ду́маю, что у него́ 4 (children). 8. В ко́мнате бы́ло семь (people), и Никола́й совсе́м не
уме́ет обраща́ться с (people). 9. Хва́лят его́ до (the skies).

17. ADJECTIVES

A. Review the <u>regular declension</u> of adjectives in the
Appendix, especially that of the "mixed" groups. The
mobile vowel О or е appears in the masculine singular of
the short adjective to separate two final consonants,
according to the same general rules as expressed in 14B.
Note, however, the rather exceptional по́лнный/по́лон, full.

B. <u>Soft Adjectives</u>. Note that <u>all</u> of these end in -ний.
(Relative adjectives of the type коро́вий, which also have
soft endings, constitute a special declensional group. See
below.) There are relatively few of them compared with
those in -ный (the most common adjective ending), and almost all of them denote position or time; i.e., they are
not qualitative adjectives, and have no short forms. The
most common are: (Positional) ве́рхний, upper; ни́жний,

lower; пере́дний, front; за́дний, rear; вне́шний, outer;
вну́тренний, inner; бли́жний, near; сосе́дний, neighboring;
да́льный, distant; also сре́дний, average; кра́йний, extreme;
(Time)дре́вний, ancient, old; пре́жний, former; после́дний,
last, latest; ра́нний, early; по́здний, late; у́тренний,
morning; вече́рний, evening; вчера́шний, of yesterday;
сего́дняшний, of today; за́втрашний, of tomorrow; весе́нний,
spring; ле́тний, summer; о́сенний, fall; зи́мний, winter.
The very few exceptions to the above two categories include дома́шний, home, domestic; и́скренний, sincere;
ли́шний, superfluous, and си́ний, (dark) blue.

C. **Adjectives Used as Nouns,** such as столо́вая, dining room;
живо́тное, animal; рабо́чий, worker, etc., and names such as
Достое́вский, Толсто́й, etc., are always declined as adjectives. (Compare the declension of names in -ов and -ин
in the Appendix.) Certain adjectives, such as учёный,
scientist, are always in the masculine, even when referring
to a woman, the understood noun being челове́к. Others,
such as ру́сский, and **especially** **names,** are in the feminine
if they refer to female persons. (For the **usage** of such
adjectives, see 46A.)

D. **Possessive Adjectives.** Review the special declensions
in the Appendix. Common examples of adjectives derived
from the names of **animals,** sometimes called "relative":
бара́ний, sheep's; во́лчий, wolf's; коро́вий, cow's; ры́бий,
fish's; соба́чий, dog's. To this group also belong ба́бий,
women's (colloq.) and бо́жий, God's. A few animal possessives, however, are formed with -иный, regularly declined,
e.g., лошади́ный, equine, horse's; similarly with зверь,
wild animal; ле́бедь, swan.

Possessives in -ин derived from nouns indicating **family**
kinship (usually feminine in form) or from first names in
-а/я, especially **diminutives,** have a colloquial and affec-
tionate character, e.g., ма́мин, Mama's; се́стрин, sister's;
дя́дин, uncle's; ба́бушкин, grandmother's; Ва́нин, Vanya's;
Ма́шин, Masha's. Others of this type expressing animal
kinship, and those in -ов/ев from masculine nouns or
names are now considered archaic and are found mainly in
certain fixed expressions, e.g., су́кин сын, son of a
bitch; ада́мово я́блоко, Adam's apple; ахилле́сова пята́,
Achilles heel.

Exercises. Translate: 1. With a new friend. 2. For the
big men. 3. In a blue room. 4. Of a blue house. 5. The
red houses. 6. Take the average woman. 7. Yesterday's
paper. 8. A black car. 9. Into the living room. 10.
Sonya is a scientist. 11. Masha will become a scientist.
12. Tanya is a Russian. 13. Mrs. Malinovsky. 14. About
Gorky. 15. With Sokolov. 16. To the animals. 17. Markov
is poor. 18. He is too slow. 19. The ocean is peaceful.
20. Ivan is kind. 21. Sonya is funny. 22. Pavel is dead.
23. The day is hot. 24. The house is full of Russians.

25. A dog's life. 26. To lead a dog's life. 27. Cow's milk. 28. God's little cow. 29. With God's help. 30. Women's summer. 31. Tchaikovsky's <u>Swan Lake</u>. 32. Solzhe- nitsyn's story "Matryona's Home" (двор). 33. Are you reading Papa's or Kolya's book? 34. I'm reading the teacher's book.

18. VERBS OF CONJUGATIONS I AND II

A. <u>Verbs in -ать</u>. The great majority of these belong to <u>Conjugation I</u> and follow the regular pattern of читáть (see Appendix). But some have a <u>consonantal stem</u>; i.e., the vowel a is dropped and the endings -у, -ет(ёт), etc., are added, e.g. ждать, wait: жду, ждёт, ждут. (Note: for convenience here and elsewhere, only the first and third person singular and the third person plural are given.) Also conjugated like ждать are врать, lie, tell lies (colloq.) and рвать, tear. For verbs in this cate- gory with consonant mutations, see 19A.

To <u>Conjugation II</u> belong a certain number of verbs whose stems end in sibilants (see 2A), among them держáть (держý, дéржит, дéржат), hold, keep; дышáть, breathe; кричáть, cry, shout; лежáть, lie; молчáть, be silent; слы́шать, hear; стучáть, knock. Note also спать (сплю, спит, спят), sleep. The greater number of verbs with the above stem consonants, however, are of Conjugation I, e.g. кончáть, end; слýшать, listen; etc.

B. <u>Verbs in -ять</u>. When this ending is preceded by a consonant, the <u>Conjugation I</u> pattern is like that of читáть, e.g. as in объяснáть, explain. When preceded by a vowel, the я is not included in the conjugation: надéяться (надéюсь, надéется, надéются), hope; смеáться (смеюсь, смеётся, смеются), laugh. The single exception is сиáть, shine brightly, which retains я: сиáю, сиáет, сиáют.

Two verbs belong to <u>Conjugation II</u>: боáться (боюсь, боится, боятся), be afraid of, and стоáть, stand.

C. <u>Verbs in -еть</u>. The majority of these, and all of those with the meaning "to become, turn," are <u>Conjugation I</u>: бледнéть (бледнéю, бледнéет, бледнéют) turn pale; грéть, warm, give warmth; жалéть, pity; краснéть, blush; смéть, dare; темнéть, grow dark; also note имéть, have; and умéть, know how.

The following belong to <u>Conjugation II</u>: горéть (горю́, горит, горáт) burn; болéть, ache (used in third person only); велéть, order; смотрéть, look, and those in 19B with consonant mutations.

D. <u>Verbs in -ить</u> are virtually without exception Conjuga- tion II, unless monosyllabic (see 20C).

E. Verbs in -овать(евать). In this fairly large group of
verbs, the -ова(ева) changes to -у (ю) in the present
tense, e.g. рисовать (рисую,рисует,рисуют), draw; воевать
(вою́ю,вою́ет,вою́ют), make war. The past is formed regularly from the infinitive: рисова́л, воева́л.

F. Verbs in -нуть. In this group, mostly perfectives, the
Conjugation I endings are added to the consonantal stem,
e.g., кри́кнуть (кри́кну,кри́кнет,кри́кнут), cry out. In the
past tense, certain verbs with stressed stems drop -ну-
and also л in the masculine singular, e.g. ги́бнуть (гиб,
ги́бла,ги́бли) perish; similarly, возни́кнуть, arise;
дости́гнуть, attain; исче́знуть, disappear; па́хнуть (imperfective) smell; привы́кнуть, become used to; замо́лкнуть,
fall silent.

G. Others. Note that the verb дуть (ду́ю, ду́ет, ду́ют),
blow; and those ending in -оть, e.g. боро́ться (борю́сь,
бо́рется, бо́рются) struggle, belong to Conjugation I.

Exercises. (a) Oral Drills. Combine subjects with verbs,
conjugating in both present (future perfective) and past:
1. I. Весь день я, ты, она́, мы, вы, они́ II. ждать друзе́й,
лежа́ть в посте́ли, слы́шать шум, слу́шать му́зыку, держа́ть
экза́мены, спать на дива́не, получа́ть телегра́ммы, молча́ть
об этом де́де, обраща́ться к ним.
2. I. Я, Ми́ша, мы, ва́ши друзья́ II. объясня́ть, наде́яться,
повторя́ть, боя́ться, объявля́ть III. что ваш брат, ва́ши
бра́тья там IV. гуля́ть, стоя́ть, изменя́ться, смея́ться,
стреля́ть
3. I. Я, ты, он, мы, вы, они́ II. си́льно бледне́ть, крас-
не́ть, горе́ть, III. когда́ смотре́ть на них, сметь проси́ть их
4. I. Вы ошиба́етесь: я, Са́ша, мы, де́вушки II. не рисо-
ва́ть вас, целова́ть вас, интересова́ться ва́ми, спра́шивать
вас, плева́ть на вас, сове́товать вам, забыва́ть вас, ноче-
ва́ть у вас, узнава́ть вас
5. I. Тут я, ты, Ма́ша, мы, вы, на́ши лю́ди II. кри́кнуть,
верну́ться, отдохну́ть, боро́ться, улыбну́ться, исче́знуть,
бледне́ть, просну́ться

(b) Supply the correct forms: 1. Мы (are waiting for)
авто́буса. 2. (We will take a rest) в э́том па́рке. 3. Ко́ля
(is demanding), чтобы мы останови́лись на сле́дующем углу́.
4. Ми́ша (kissed) Та́ню, когда́ они́ (danced). 5. Лев (is
showing) нам свой сад, хотя́ он (feels) себя́ нева́жно. 6.
А́ня (is interested) кинозвё́здами. 7. Мы слы́шали, как
больна́я (cried out). 8. Как то́лько (arose) вопро́сы, наш
това́рищ (disappeared). 9. Ива́н (smiled), потому́ что цветы́
(smelled) так прия́тно. 10. Я вам не (advise) с ни́ми спо́р-
ить. Вы уже́ (tearing) бума́гу. 11. Ка́ждый день лю́ди (perish), но Па́вел никогда́ не (will get used) к э́тому фа́кту.
12. "Ты (lying)," сказа́л Гри́ша, и (fell silent). 13. Ната́ша
(returned) то́лько вчера́, и уже́ (is finishing) свою́ рабо́ту.

(c) Translate: 1. They look and listen, but they don't see or hear. 2. I'm sorry your head aches. 3. Tanya and Masha are sleeping, but Varya is lying there and shouting. 4. I hope it gets dark soon. 5. Why do you blush when the boys shout? 6. Vanya didn't laugh. He didn't even breathe. 7. They don't dare come in, because they're afraid of him. 8. We are holding the packages in our arms and knocking on the door. Nobody answers. 9. Since he doesn't know how to say this in Russian, he keeps quiet. 10. We sit by the window and watch the birds fly. 11. The wind is blowing and the sun shines brightly in the sky. 12. The president stood where you are standing now. 13. "We are struggling with them," he says. 14. "We are at war with them, and we will attain victory!"

19. VERBS WITH CONSONANT MUTATIONS

These occur in verbs with <u>consonantal stems</u>, including some of Conjugation I in -ать (e.g. пис-а́ть as opposed to чита́-ть) and many of Conjugation II (e.g. ход-и́ть, also ви́д-еть as opposed to Conj. I уме́-ть), according to the following regular mutations: д, з > ж; к, т > ч (in a few cases т > щ); с, х > ш; ск, ст > щ; б, в, м, п, ф (the labial consonants) > бл, вл, мл, пл, фл.

A. <u>Conjugation I</u>. The mutations occur <u>throughout</u> the present tense and in the imperative and present participles, e.g. писа́ть, write: пишу́, пи́шет, пи́шут; пиши́(те), пи́шущий. Other common examples: (з > ж): вяза́ть, tie, bind; ре́зать, cut; сказа́ть, say, tell; (к, т > ч): пла́кать, weep; скака́ть, jump, gallop; бормота́ть, mutter; пря́тать, hide; хохота́ть, guffaw; шепта́ть, whisper; (с, х > ш): пляса́ть, dance (folk or informal); колыха́ться, sway; маха́ть, wave; паха́ть, plow; (ск > щ): иска́ть, look for; (б, м, п > бл, мл, пл): колеба́ться, waver, hesitate; дрема́ть, doze; трепа́ть, flutter.

B. <u>Conjugation II</u>. Here mutations occur only in the <u>first person singular</u> and the <u>past passive participle</u>. In the latter, sometimes д > жд, e.g. роди́ть, give birth: рожу́, роди́т, родя́т; рождённый. Other common examples, most of them in -ить but some in -еть: (д > ж): буди́ть, awaken; ви́деть, see; води́ть, lead; е́здить, go, ride; сади́ться, sit down; сиде́ть, be sitting; серди́ться, be angry; ходи́ть, go; (з > ж): вози́ть, convey; скользи́ть, slip, skid; (т > ч): встре́тить, meet; лете́ть, fly; отве́тить, answer; плати́ть, pay; шути́ть, joke; (т > щ): обрати́ть(ся), turn; посвяти́ть, devote; (с > ш): бро́сить, throw; носи́ть, carry; пригласи́ть, invite; проси́ть ask (a favor); (ст > щ): прости́ть, forgive; пусти́ть, let; свисте́ть, whistle; чи́стить, clean; (б > бл): люби́ть, love; руби́ть, chop; (в > вл): гото́вить, prepare, cook; лови́ть, catch; ста́вить, put, stand; станови́ться, become; (м > мл): знако́мить, acquaint; корми́ть, feed; шуме́ть, make noise; (п > пл): купи́ть, buy; терпе́ть, endure.

The verb спать, sleep (сплю, спит, спят) also belongs
here. N.B. all of the verbs listed in A and a majority
of those in B which have a stressed infinitive ending
have __mobile stress__ in the present tense of the type пишу́,
пи́шет, пи́шут (see 21C).

__Exercises.__ (a) Combine subjects with verbs in present:
1. Почему́ я, ты, он, мы, вы, они́ (пла́кать, пляса́ть, дре-
ма́ть, шепта́ть, исчеза́ть, колеба́ться) пока́ ты, я, они́, вы,
он, мы (писа́ть, чита́ть, иска́ть, вяза́ть, броса́ть, пря́тать)
пи́сьма?
2. Ка́ждый день ле́том я, Ва́ля, бра́тья (ходи́ть, е́здить) в
дере́вню, (води́ть, вози́ть, носи́ть) Ко́лю на о́зеро и там
с ним (спать, шути́ть, шуме́ть, сади́ться на бе́рег, сиде́ть
на берегу́, лови́ть, чи́стить, и гото́вить ры́бу)
3. Кто (ви́деть, встре́тить, корми́ть, люби́ть, прости́ть, при-
гласи́ть, разбуди́ть, спроси́ть) его́? Я, они́ (---) его́.
(b) Supply the correct forms: 1. Что вы (looking for)?
Я (looking for) че́стного челове́ка. Но оди́н дре́вний грек
до́лго (looked for) че́стного челове́ка, и не нашёл ни одного́.
2. Не (cry), он тебе́ (will tell), что де́лать. 3. Со́ня
(is dozing), пока́ все круго́м (make noise). 4. Я (will
buy) это пла́тье, так как я не (see) лу́чшего. 5. Брат
(laughs loud), когда́ я говорю́, что я (will devote) свою́
жизнь нау́ке. 6. Где вы (sleep)? --Обы́чно я (sleep) внутри́
до́ма, но вчера́ но́чью я (slept) на дворе́. 7. Если вы мне
(tell) "нет", то я (will turn) к Светло́ву. 8. Пти́цы уже́
(are flying) на юг. 9. "Я то́лько (kidding)," говори́т
Са́ша. "Я не (clean) его́ боти́нок." 10. Га́ля (is crying) и
(saying), что она́ никогда́ не (will forgive) тебе́. 11.
Когда́ я (meet) его́ за́втра, я (will ask) его́ об э́том, но он,
вероя́тно, (won't answer) на мой вопро́с. 12. Я (won't let)
тебя́ (invite) его́ на вечери́нку, потому́ что он всё вре́мя
(jumps) как ло́шадь по ко́мнате. 13. Она́ (cuts) хлеб и мя́со
и (feeds) всех люде́й, кото́рых она́ (sees). Они́ ей не (pay).
14. Весно́й па́харь (plows) зе́млю и се́ет, и ле́том (sways)
рожь на ветру́. 15. "Лес (they cut)--ще́пки (fly)."

20. "IRREGULAR" VERBS

The heading of this section appears in quotation marks
because when all predictable changes in stems are taken
into account, there are actually very few irregular verbs
in Russian. For a full demonstration of the language's
surprising degree of regularity in this respect, see
Charles E. Townsend, __Russian Word Formation__ (New York,
1968), pp. 81-114: "Single Basic Stem and Form: Classifi-
cation and Conjugation". With only one exception (not
counting those of "mixed" conjugation in D), the verbs
given below belong to __Conjugation I__.

A. Verbs with Infinitive Ending Preceded by a Consonant.
Those in -сти and -сть have three different possible stem
consonants. Note the с in нести́, carry (несу́, несёт,
несу́т) and спасти́, save (perfective); the т in цвести́,
bloom (цвету́, цветёт, цвету́т) and both in расти́, grow
(расту́, растёт, расту́т). Others have д: вести́, lead
(веду́, ведёт, веду́т); класть, put; красть, steal; упа́сть,
fall (perf.) Note the vowel change in сесть, sit down
(perf.): ся́ду, ся́дет, ся́дут. Идти́ also belongs here:
иду́, идёт, иду́т. In prefixed forms of this verb, и > й,
e.g. найти́, find: найду́, найдёт, найду́т. Verbs in -зти
(-зть) have the stem consonant з, e.g. везти́, convey:
везу́, везёт, везу́т; лезть, climb: ле́зу, ле́зет, ле́зут.

In the **past tense**, verbs with stems in т or д drop these
consonants, e.g. вести́/вёл, вела́, вели́. The masculine
singular has ё; an important exception is сесть/сел.
The past of идти́ is quite irregular: шёл, шла, шло, шли.
Verbs with other stem consonants retain these at the ex-
pense of the л in the masculine singular, e.g. нести́/
нёс, несла́, несли́. Note the vowel change in расти́: рос,
росла́, росли.

B. Verbs in -чь have consonant alternations within the
present tense, before the endings in -е: either г > ж as
in мочь, be able (могу́, мо́жет, мо́гут); жечь, burn (жгу,
жжёт, жгут), and лечь, lie down (perf., ля́гу, ля́жет,
ля́гут; note the vowel change); or к > ч as in печь, bake
(пеку́, печёт, пеку́т); and, similarly, течь, flow. Also
belonging to this conjugational type is лгать, (tell a)
lie, which has лгу, лжёт, лгут.

In the **past tense**, the г or к is retained and л is dropped
in the masculine singular, e.g. мог, могла́, могли́. Note
жечь/жёг, жгла, жгли. The past of лгать is regularly
formed from the infinitive: лгал, лгала́, лга́ли.

C. Verbs with Unpredictable Stem Changes. Note the following **alternations**: и > ь in бить, beat (бью, бьёт, бьют);
similarly in уби́ть, kill (perf.); вить, wind (разви́ть,
develop, perf.); лить, pour; пить drink; шить, sew. The
imperatives of these verbs are in -ей: бей(те), пей(те),
etc.; ы > о in крыть, cover (кро́ю, кро́ет, кро́ют); similarly in закры́ть, close, and откры́ть, open (perfs.); выть,
howl; мыть(ся), wash; ныть, ache; рыть(ся) dig; е > о in
петь, sing (пою́, поёт, пою́т); х > д in е́хать, go, ride
(е́ду, е́дет, е́дут); с > ш in слать, send (шлю, шлёт, шлют);
usually found in prefixed perfectives such as посла́ть,
присла́ть.

Note the following **losses**: of -ва- in дава́ть, give (даю́,
даёт, даю́т); similarly in prefixed forms such as подава́ть,
serve; продава́ть, sell; and in forms of -знава́ть (e.g.
узнава́ть, recognize) and -става́ть (e.g. встава́ть get up);

but N.B. that the imperative as well as the present gerund and passive participle retain it, e.g. дава́й(те), дава́я, дава́емый; of e in forms of -мере́ть, die (e.g. умере́ть (умру́, умрёт, умру́т, past у́мер, умерла́, у́мерли); similarly in -пере́ть (e.g. запере́ть, lock; past за́пер, заперла́, за́перли), and тере́ть, rub (past тёр, тёрла, тёрли)

<u>Stem vowels and consonants not appearing in infinitive:</u> е in брать, take (беру́, берёт, беру́т); similarly in дра́ться, fight; о in звать, call (зову́, зовёт, зову́т); note also in Conjugation II гнать, drive, chase (гоню́, го́нит, го́нят); в in жить, live (живу́, живёт, живу́т); similarly in плыть, swim; м in the perfectives поня́ть, understand (пойму́, поймёт, пойму́т); similarly in заня́ть, occupy; приня́ть, accept, receive (приму́, при́мет, при́мут), снять, take off, rent (сниму́, сни́мет, сни́мут) similarly in подня́ть, raise; also note взять, take (возьму́, возьмёт, возьму́т); н in the perfectives нача́ть(ся), begin (начну́, начнёт(ся), начну́т(ся); оде́ть(ся), dress (оде́ну(сь), оде́нет(ся), оде́нут(ся)); стать, begin, become (ста́ну, ста́нет, ста́нут).

<u>D. Verbs of Special or Mixed Conjugation</u> (the only ones fully deserving of the term "irregular") include бежа́ть, run (бегу́, бежи́т, бегу́т); хоте́ть, want (хочу́, хо́чет; хоти́м, хотя́т); есть, eat (ем, ешь, ест, еди́м, еди́те, едя́т, imperative ешь); дать, give (perf., дам, даш, даст, дади́м, дади́те, даду́т, imperative дай). Of быть, to be, the only present tense form used is есть; the future is бу́ду, бу́дет, бу́дут.

<u>Exercises.</u> Oral Drills. 1. Я, он, мы, они́ (вести́, везти́, нести́) ребёнка на пло́щадь и сам/са́ми туда́ (стать в о́чередь, сесть, лечь).
2. Кто из вас (пить, откры́ть, дава́ть на, узнава́ть, брать взять, приня́ть) во́дку? --Я, мы, они́ (---).
3. Я, ты, Стёпа, мы, вы, го́сти не (хоте́ть, есть, дать ему́) апельси́нов.

Supply the correct forms: 1. Сего́дня дя́дя (is taking) Ко́лю в го́род, а за́втра он (will take) тебя́. 2. Учи́тельница (will accept) ва́шу отгово́рку е́сли она́ её (will understand). 3. Почему́ Со́ня не (eat), когда́ други́е (eat)? 4. Е́сли вы (want), я (will give) вам знать, когда́ он (dies). 5. Он никогда́ не (drinks) ко́фе. (Нали́ть) ему́, пожа́луйста, ча́ю. 6. Вы всегда́ (beat) жену́? --О, нет! Вчера́ я ни ра́зу не (beat) её. 7. Её (they call) Еле́ной. Она́ (lives) в э́том зда́нии. 8. Оте́ц (is driving) свине́й в хлев и (singing). 9. За́втра мы (will get up) ра́но, потому́ что заня́тия (will begin) в во́семь часо́в. 10. Фе́дя (is running) в лес и они́ (are running) за ним.

Translate: 1. Who stole my coat? 2. She won't sit down
here. 3. The flowers are in bloom, but the vegetables
aren't growing. 4. We were going to the theater. 5. He
was carrying a large package into the house. 6. Can you
burn these boxes? I've been burning them all day. 7.
Either sit down or lie down. 8. Where are you leading
us? 9. She couldn't open the door. 10. Tanya read the
magazine yesterday. 11. Trees never grow here. 12. We
usually put our things into a box. 13. I found the package but will not open it. 14. The river flows through
town. 15. Every day they bake bread. 16. If I fall into
the water, will you save me? 17. If I fell into the water
would you save me? 18. No, I couldn't save you. 19. I'll
get dressed and then I'll close the window. 20. If
you're lying, I'll kill you. 21. He doesn't recognize
you. 22. Their father died four years ago.

21. STRESS PATTERNS

A. Nouns. In general, the stress is fixed on the same
syllable throughout the declension as the nominative
singular when it is medial (i.e., not initial or final)
in nouns of more than two syllables, e.g. рассказчик,
создание, болото. It is fixed in feminine nouns in -а
(я) when the stress is not final, e.g. комната, неделя.
But the following patterns of shift, with common examples,
are to be noted:

Stress on endings in singular and plural (masculine nouns
only), e.g. стол, table: sing. стола, столу, etc., plural
столы, столов, etc. Other monosyllabic nouns: вождь,
leader; враг, enemy; врач, physician; двор, yard; дождь,
rain; ключ, key; нож, knife; Пётр, Peter; рубль, ruble;
труд, labor; ум, mind; царь, tsar. Nouns ending in
stressed syllables or suffixes in -к, the sibilants, and
-арь belong to this category, e.g. дурак, fool (gen. sg.
дурака); similarly богач, rich man; гараж, garage; кир-
пич, brick; карандаш, pencil; кузнец. blacksmith; ученик,
pupil; словарь, dictionary; этаж, floor, story; язык,
tongue, language. Other polysyllabic nouns include кор-
абль, ship; король, king; топор, axe; угол, corner;
четверг, Thursday; note also the months январь, февраль;
сентябрь through декабрь.

The nouns ряд, row; час, hour; шаг, step, pace, take
stressed а in the genitive singular after the numerals
2, 3, 4: два часа, три шага, etc. Numerals in -ь, although declined as feminine nouns, have stressed endings,
e.g. с пятью мальчиками, with five boys.

Stress on plural endings only, e.g. нос, nose, sing. носа,
носу, etc., but pl. носы, носов, etc. Masculine nouns include those taking stressed locative -у (ю) (see 12A) and
the -а(я) nominative plural (see 15A). In neuter nouns

of usually not more than two syllables with a stressed
first syllable in the singular, the stress is regularly
on the endings in the plural, e.g. де́ло, matter, business
(pl. дела́, дел, дела́м, etc.); зе́ркало, mirror; ме́сто,
place; мо́ре, sea; по́ле, field; сло́во, word.

Stress on oblique plural endings only, that is, beginning
with the genitive, e.g. дверь, door, nom. pl. две́ри, but
gen. двере́й, dat. дверя́м, etc. This group consists mainly of nouns in -ь of either gender: вещь, thing; гость,
guest; ка́мень, stone; кость, bone; ло́шадь, horse; но́вость,
news; ночь, night; речь, speech; тень, shadow; це́рковь,
church; часть, part. Note the stressed "locative" singular in certain nouns of this type, e.g. на двери́, on the
door; в крови́, in the blood; в связи́ (с), in connection
(with); в степи́ in the steppe; в тени́, in the shade.
This parallels the masculine "locative" singular in -у́(ю́).

Stress moves back. In neuter nouns with final stress in
singular, it regularly moves back one syllable throughout
the plural, e.g. лицо́, face (nom. pl. ли́ца); окно́, window;
перо́, feather, pen (пе́рья); ружье́, gun; число́, number.
Note that e is usually ё in the plural, e.g. колесо́, wheel
(колёса). Feminine nouns with final stress generally show
a similar pattern, e.g., глава́, chapter, head; дыра́, hole;
жена́, wife (жёны); звезда́, star (ё); игра́, game;
сестра́, sister (ё, but gen. сестёр); страна́, country.

There is a special group in which the accusative singular
and nominative plural only have initial stress (that of
the oblique plural usually falling on the endings), e.g.
рука́, hand, arm: acc. sg. ру́ку, nom. pl. ру́ки, but dat.
pl. рука́м. Others: борода́, beard (бо́роду); вода́, water;
голова́, head; гора́, hill, mountain; доска́, board; душа́,
soul; земля́, earth; зима́, winter; нога́, leg, foot; река́,
river; спина́, back; среда́, Wednesday; стена́, wall;
сторона́, side; цена́, price; щека́, cheek (щёку).

B. Adjectives. The stress is always fixed throughout the
declension of the long form, and it is usually fixed also
in the short forms of adjectives of three or more syllables, e.g. краси́вый, beautiful: краси́в, краси́ва, краси́вы.
Mobility occurs regularly only in the short forms of two-
syllable adjectives, in which the stress moves onto the
ending of the feminine, e.g., бе́дный, poor: бе́ден, бедна́.
But this is also true of certain three-syllable adjectives,
e.g. высо́кий, high; глубо́кий, deep; далёкий, far; за́нятый,
busy; широ́кий, wide.

In a few adjectives of three syllables with middle or
final stress, the feminine ending is stressed while the
other forms show an initial stress, e.g. весёлый, happy,
gay (ве́сел, весела́, ве́селы); similarly, голо́дный, hungry;
дешёвый, cheap (дёшев); дорого́й, dear, expensive; молодо́й,
young; холо́дный, cold.

In the following, the stress is <u>final</u> on the neuter and plural as well as the feminine short endings: больно́й, ill (бо́лен, больна́, больны́); горя́чий, hot; ра́вный, equal; смешно́й, funny (смешо́н); тяжёлый, heavy; у́мный, smart (умён); хоро́ший, good (-looking).

C. <u>Verbs</u>. In verbs with a vowel stem (Conjugation I, e.g. чита́ть) the stress is always fixed in present and past. It is also fixed in verbs with consonant stems having infinitives of more than one syllable in which the <u>stem</u> is stressed, e.g., ста́вить. But note:

<u>Present</u>: The stress may be mobile in verbs with consonant stems having a <u>stressed infinitive ending</u>. In this case, the stress is final in the first person singular only and moves back one syllable in all other persons, e.g. писа́ть: пишу́, пи́шешь, пи́шет, пи́шем, etc. A general rule is that verbs of this type with <u>consonant mutations</u> have this stress shift; this is true of all the Conjugation I verbs and the great majority of Conjugation II verbs listed in Section 19. Other common examples: держа́ть, hold; дыша́ть, breathe; мочь, be able; положи́ть, put; получи́ть, get; смотре́ть, look; учи́ть(ся), study; хоте́ть, want (but in plural хоти́м, хоти́те, хотя́т).

<u>Past</u>: In a number of monosyllabic verbs, the <u>feminine</u> ending takes the stress while the other stresses remain initial: быть, to be (был, была́, бы́ло, бы́ли); брать and взять, take; дать, give; ждать, wait; жить, live; звать, call; лгать, lie; лить, pour; пить, drink; плыть, swim; рвать, tear; спать, sleep.

The same is true of prefixed forms of these verbs, and in certain cases the stress is on the <u>prefix</u> except in the feminine; note those in -дать, e.g. зада́ть, put (a question); пода́ть, serve; прода́ть, sell (про́дал, продала́, про́дали); also in -нять, e.g. поня́ть, understand; приня́ть, accept; and нача́ть(ся) begin (на́чал, начала́, на́чали, but начался́, начала́сь, начали́сь); умере́ть, die.

In a similar pattern, the stress moves onto the negative particle не when it is used with the past tense of быть, дать, and жить, except in the feminine, e.g. не́ был, не была́, не́ было, не́ были.

<u>Exercises</u>. Oral drills. 1. Combine prepositions with nouns where appropriate in both <u>singular and plural</u>: Сего́дня я хожу́ без, к, по, с (америка́нец, башма́к, бога́ч, го́род, двор, дом, до́ктор, дура́к, Ива́н, каранда́ш, ключ, кора́бль, кузне́ц, лес, мост, мужи́к, нож, оте́ц, паке́т, Пётр, рубль, сад, спу́тник, стари́к, стол, труд, учени́к, фона́рь, челове́к)
2. Decline properly in <u>plural</u>: Что вы ду́маете о (боло́то, де́ло, зе́ркало, зда́ние, коле́но, колесо́, лицо́, ме́сто, мо́ре, о́блако, одея́ло, окно́, перо́, письмо́, плечо́, по́ле, ра́дио,

ружьё, слово, у́хо, число, яйцо́)?
3. Decline where feasible in **singular and plural**:
Стре́лы попа́ли в / куда́-то ме́жду (борода́, вода́, голова́, гора́, госпожа́, гость, дверь, доска́, дочь, дыра́, жена́, звезда́, земля́, ка́рта, коро́бка, ло́шадь, мать, нога́, по́езд, река́, рука́, сестра́, соба́ка, стена́)
4. Combine subjects with proper **short forms** of adjectives:
Говоря́т, что Ва́ня, Та́ня, де́вушки (больно́й, весёлый, винова́тый, голо́дный, гото́вый, за́нятый, молодо́й, пра́вый, рад, свобо́дный, смешно́й, хоро́ший)
5. Supply the proper forms of the **past tense**:
Кто из вас (брать, взять, дать, ждать, знать, нести́, откры́ть, рвать, поня́ть, приня́ть, прода́ть, мочь--нача́ть--стать--хоте́ть чита́ть) э́ту статью́?   --Она́, мы (---).

Translate and stress correctly: 1. There is no rain.
2. Under the rain. 3. 3 pencils. 4. 6 pencils. 5. In
February. 6. In March. 7. In November. 8. 4 rubles.
9. 5 rubles. 10. On the ship. 11. 3 guests. 12. 10
guests. 13. No news. 14. Words of the Russian language.
15. How are things going? 16. In this place. 17. In
these places. 18. 3 letters. 19. 8 letters. 20. Into
the field. 21. Into the fields. 22. In the buildings.
23. In your blood. 24. Across the street. 25. On Wednesday. 26. To the other side. 27. We read the fifth chapter. 28. About their wives. 29. The reports of six
students. 30. With 10 men. 31. The houses are new.
32. The room is new. 33. The gift is expensive. 34. The
hat is expensive. 35. These hats are cheap. 36. The
Volga is wide and deep. 37. Here the work is heavy.
38. What will you tell him? 39. I'll tell him no. 40.
They won't take off their hats. 41. I will get a new
watch. What will you get? 42. They will put the books
on the shelves. 43. I can't do this, but you can. 44.
She was drinking and singing. 45. She lived, slept and
washed here. 46. We were never there. 47. We never
lived there. 48. The concert began at 8:00.

SUPPLEMENTARY TRANSLATION EXERCISE: One of the last
stories I read was "The Black Cat" by (of) Edgar Allan
Poe. Reading such a story is like sitting in the movies
and watching Frankenstein or Dracula. The narrator (рас-
ска́зчик), who does not give his name, says that he always
liked animals. He liked birds and fish too, but most of
all he liked Pluto, his cat. Then he began to drink...
he drinks too much and beats his wife and his cat. Finally he kills the poor animal. Doctors and professors of
psychology, he thinks, cannot explain why he did it.
Such a man has no friends, and it is a good thing that he
has no children. He is sorry and looks for another cat.
He finds a cat that looks like Pluto: it is black and
has lost one of its eyes. It likes him and is always on
his trousers or overcoat. At first he is interested in
this cat but later is afraid of it because he remembers

the first one. He wants to kill it; his wife argues but
he is holding an axe. Suddenly she is lying on the floor
with the axe in her forehead. He buries (хоронить) her
in a pile of bricks. But he makes a mistake and buries
the cat too. Later the cat is still alive and screams
(use кричать), telling the police where to find the
corpse. Of course, they will arrest (арестовать, perf.)
him. As the narrator said at the beginning of the story,
"Tomorrow I die."

22. NOMINATIVE CASE

A. <u>Basic Usages</u>. These are similar to English; that is,
for the subject of the sentence and its modifiers, direct
address, predicate nominative. A not infrequent mistake
of the first-year student is to use the nominative for
the first word in a question when the accusative or other
case is required, e.g. *кто (for кого) вы видите, Who(m)
do you see? Another is to treat a linking verb such as
"to be" as transitive (i.e., one taking a direct object)
and put the predicate into the accusative, e.g. это была
*мою учительницу rather than the correct моя учительница,
that was my teacher. Also note well that while the ob-
jective case of a pronoun instead of the predicate nominative is now acceptable in English (e.g. "it is me")
and is the rule in French (<u>c'est moi</u>), the nominative
must be used in Russian: это я. However, the <u>instrument-
al</u> is also used with the predicate nominative in certain
instances; see 27B.

B. <u>Apposition</u>. Titles of artistic works, periodicals,
buildings, projects, etc., following a generic noun in
an oblique case remain in the nominative: я читаю "Войну
и мир", I am reading <u>War and Peace</u>, but я читаю <u>роман</u>
"Война и мир", I am reading the <u>novel</u> War and Peace.
The same is generally true of place names: в Нью Йорке,
in New York, but в штате Нью Йорк, in the <u>state</u> (of) New
York; although with names of cities declension is also
possible: в городе Москва or Москве, in the city (of)
Moscow. Note here also the vacillation of usage with
the formula меня (его, её) зовут..., they call me (him,
her)...: the instrumental is still considered correct,
but the nominative is quite acceptable and probably more
often used, e.g. его зовут Роберт as well as Робертом,
his name is Robert.

C. <u>Usage with Prepositions</u>. The idiom что за, a more
colloquial alternative to какой in the meaning of "what
(sort of)" is an interesting and unique instance in which
the preposition is followed not by the expected oblique
case but by the nominative: что за учитель Грибов? What
kind of teacher is Gribov?; что за погода! what (bad)
weather! It may also be noted here that the nominative-
rather than the normal genitive-accusative plural form

of an animate noun is used in certain fixed phrases with
the preposition в; among the most common are ходи́ть в
го́сти, go visiting, and выходи́ть в лю́ди, come up in the
world.

Exercises. Translate: 1. Who are you talking to, Misha?
2. Who are you talking to? Misha? 3. No, I'm talking
to you, Vanya! 4. I'm talking to my sister Masha. 5.
I don't care what you say--truth is truth. 6. Here's a
lamp for you. 7. Sonya was a very good woman. 8. Who
knows Professor Zubov? 9. Who does Professor Zubov know?
10. What book are you reading? 11. I'm reading the play
Uncle Vanya. 12. What sort of play is that? 13. Where
are you going? Moscow? 14. That's in Three Sisters.
15. What state do you live in? --In the state of Michigan. 16. Well, I live in Wisconsin, city of Madison.
17. Call me Matt. 18. They say there's no truth in
Pravda; that is, in the newspaper Pravda. 19. If you
want to find the truth, look for it at the bottom of
Lake Baikal, at the top of Mt. Everest, or in The Brothers Karamazov. 20. I'm not going to look for anything;
I'm just going visiting.

23. ACCUSATIVE AND PREPOSITIONAL CASES

A. Accusative. Review the regular endings in the Appendix, noting that the accusative has an ending of its own
only in the singular of feminine nouns in -a(я). Otherwise, the nominative endings are used for inanimate nouns
and their modifiers, and the genitive for animate (10B).

In addition to its basic usage as the direct object of a
verb, the accusative indicates the time or distance
covered by an action, e.g. рабо́тать всю неде́лю, to work
all week; пройти́ пять миль to walk five miles. (For the
usage of the accusative in other time expressions, see
Sections 50-51.) It may also indicate cost, e.g. сто́ить
рубль, to cost a ruble.

B. Prepositions with the Accusative. The accusative is
used with the following prepositions when motion is indicated: в (во before certain consonant clusters such as
вс, вт, мн), to, into (note also: игра́ть в ка́рты, те́ннис,
etc., to play cards, tennis, etc.); на, to, onto (note
the expressions, with an idea of motion involved, смотре́ть
на, look at; серди́ться на, be angry at; опа́здывать на,
be late for; быть похо́жим на, look like, resemble, with
the adjective normally used in its short forms); за,
behind, beyond (note the idioms за́ город, out of town;
за грани́цу, abroad; and the meaning of "for" in спаси́бо
за, thanks for; плати́ть за, pay for; голосова́ть за, vote
for, etc.); под, under. When these prepositions indicate
location rather than motion, в and на take the prepositional (see C below), while за and под take the instru-

mental (see 27D). The prepositions че́рез, across, through, and сквозь, through (in the sense of penetrating) are also used with the accusative.

C. **Prepositional Case.** Review the endings, noting those masculine nouns which have -у́(ю́) after в and на (see 12A). This case is used only with prepositions: в and на when position "in, on, at" is indicated (compare я рабо́таю в го́роде, I work in the city, with я е́ду в го́род, I am going to the city, in which the difference between location and motion is expressed in English by using different prepositions. Note also игра́ть на роя́ле, на скри́пке, etc., to play the piano, violin, etc., and expressions concerning the marriage of men: Никола́й жени́лся (жена́т) на Ма́рфе, Nikolay married (is married to) Martha). The preposition О, about, concerning, takes the form об before words beginning with a **vowel** **sound** (об Ива́не, об уро́ке, but **not** *об Евро́пе, and обо before certain consonant clusters: обо мне, обо всем, etc.) The preposition при has various meanings: при Ива́не, in Ivan's presence; при университе́те, with, attached to the university; при хоро́шей пого́де, in the case of, given good weather; при Петре́ I, in the time, reign of Peter I. For the usage of the prepositional in **time expressions**, see 50-51.

D. **Special Distinction between в and на.** In the meanings of "into, to" and "in, at," в is normally used when the object is a concrete indoor place (e.g. банк, кино́, теа́тр) a city or country (Москва́, Аме́рика), or anything that can enclose (река́, тума́н), and на when it is an open place or flat surface (пло́щадь, эта́ж), a point of the compass (за́пад, восто́к, се́вер, юг), or an activity or occasion (ле́кция, собра́ние, обе́д). Also note the expressions на дворе́, на у́лице, outside, out of doors, and the difference between на углу́, on the corner (outside), and в углу́, in the corner (inside). However, certain nouns, notably заво́д, plant; фа́брика, factory; по́чта, post office; ры́нок, market; вокза́л, terminal, and ста́нция, station, even though today they usually represent enclosed places, take на instead of в.

Exercises. Oral Drills: 1. Decline in singular and plural: Па́па мне даёт (пода́рок, одея́ло, ку́кла, медве́дь, ло́шадь, после́дняя фотогра́фия, чёрная ко́шка)
2. Combine verbs with objects and their proper prepositions: Сего́дня мы идём, бы́ли в / на (банк, го́род, заво́д, кино́, клуб, ле́кция, о́пера, парк, по́чта, пя́тый эта́ж, собра́ние, ста́нция, теа́тр, фа́брика, фильм, шко́ла)
3. Combine verbs with objects where possible: А́нна смо́трит, се́рдится, опа́здывает, игра́ет, похо́жа, кладёт журна́лы, стои́т на (оте́ц, мать, дя́дя, авто́бус, собра́ние, бабала́йка, роя́ль, стол)
4. Decline, with the correct form of the preposition: Па́ша всё вре́мя говори́т о (ты, мы, они́, я, америка́нцы,

Евгений, пустяки, языки, иностранные языки, новая машина, этот дом, это здание, свои карты, своё пальто, всё и все)

Supply the correct forms: 1. Сергей ест (bread), но не ест (meat). 2. Светлов убил (своя жена), (свой друг), и затем (himself). 3. Я знаю (все) их (отцы) и (матери). 4. Пойдём в (это здание). 5. Мы живём в (большой дом) на (широкая улица). 6. Саша идёт в (сад). 7. Сестра гуляет в (сад). 8. Не сердитесь на (me). 9. Расскажите мне о (собрание). 10. Ты думаешь (about me) или (about him)? 11. Собака бежит под (диван). 12. Кошка лежит под (диван). 13. Если мы начнём играть сейчас, то я опоздаю на (лекция). 14. Он пробегает (миля) каждый день. 15. Три поросёнка шли (to market). 16. Сколько вы платите за (эта комната)? 17. Они все похожи на (своя мать). 18. Это случилось при (Екатерина Вторая).

Translate: 1. I saw you at the concert, but I didn't see her. 2. I'm going to the lecture, and then to the movies. 3. Do you know the lesson? 4. Do you know this doctor? 5. No, but I know his father. 6. Mary is reading a difficult book. 7. I'm taking Mary to the post office, and then to the theater. 8. We danced all night. 9. Why are you putting the sugar on the table? 10. Look at Sergey! He's dancing on the table. 11. Susan is angry with her friends. 12. Thanks for your help. 13. Excuse me for the trouble (беспокойство). 14. Are you thinking about the exam? 15. I'm not going to the exam. 16. Look at that store across the street. 17. I couldn't see through the rain. 18. Do you want to play chess with me? 19. No, I want to play the violin. 20. Smith is going out of town. 21. Smith is out of town today. 22. This pencil costs only a kopeck. 23. The Eskimos (эскимосы) live in the north. 24. Don't say that with Sasha around. 25. I want to write about your brother. 26. Your brother married a good woman.

24. GENITIVE CASE I

A. **Possession.** Note that in this basic usage of the genitive, the possessor, indicated in English with "'s", **follows** the thing possessed in Russian: Ivan's house is дом Ивана, **not** *Ивана дом, a fairly frequent mistake. Compare the usage of possessive adjectives, which have limited possibilities in standard modern Russian (17D). In most contexts, the English "of" is rendered simply by the genitive without a preposition: директор музея, director of a museum; стакан вина, a glass of wine; карта Европы, a map of Europe; etc. But note the use of simply two nouns in apposition in город Москва, the city of Moscow; сентябрь месяц the month of September, etc., and the use of **adjectives** in московский университет, University of Moscow; английский король, king of England, and in similar constructions. On the other hand, N.B. geography lesson, уро́к геогра́фии; Russian teacher, учи́тель ру́сского языка́ (ру́сский учи́тель would mean, literally, a teacher who is Russian). Also note such constructions as како́го цве́та э́то пла́тье?, (of) what color is the dress?

B. Quantity. After adverbs such as ско́лько, how much; мно́го, much, many; ма́ло, little, few; не́сколько, several, a few; доста́точно (недоста́точно), sufficient, enough (not enough); бо́льше, more; ме́ньше, fewer, less, the genitive **singular** is used with nouns of a collective nature (e.g. ско́лько воды́, хле́ба, how much water, bread) while the **plural** is used with things that can be counted (e.g. ско́лько столо́в, ко́мнат how many tables, rooms). When "some" rather than "all" of a thing is implied, the genitive rather than the accusative is used: да́йте мне мя́со, give me <u>the</u> meat, but да́йте мне мя́са, give me <u>some</u> meat. This usage is common with verbs such as хоте́ть and купи́ть: хочу́ ча́ю, I want (some) tea; она́ купи́ла хле́ба, she bought (some) bread. The basic quantitative usage of the genitive extends to numerals and comparisons (see Sections 47-49).

C. Negation. As a rule, the direct object of a negated verb is in the genitive, e.g. он не зна́ет уро́ка, he doesn't know the lesson. But there appears to be considerable vacillation of usage in contemporary Russian between the genitive and the accusative, much of it on stylistic grounds. See F. M. Borras and R. F. Christian, <u>Russian Syntax</u>, second edition, Oxford, 1971, pp. 28-31, and Dennis Ward, <u>The Russian Language Today</u>, Chicago, 1965, pp. 211-221. According to the theory expressed by Ward, the genitive tends to be used if the emphasis is on the object, the accusative if on the verb, e.g. он не покупа́ет кни́ги, he is not buying the <u>book</u> (but something else); он не покупа́ет кни́гу, he is not <u>buying</u> the book (but just browsing).

Note that the accusative will definitely be used if the particle не negates a word other than the verb: не я разби́л таре́лку, it was not I who broke the plate; они́ не всё зна́ют, they don't know everything. And, of course, он не до́ктор, not *он не до́ктора, since here "doctor" is simply a predicate nominative rather than the object of a verb.

Нет, in the meaning "there is (are) no" (a contraction of не + есть, past always не́ было, future always не бу́дет, regardless of gender or number) is always followed by the genitive, e.g. здесь нет сту́льев, there are no chairs here; в я́щике не́ было бума́ги, there was no paper in the drawer; на собра́нии не бу́дет же́нщин, there will be no women at the meeting.

Exercises. **Oral Drills.** 1. **Decline:** Вам нравится цвет (наш дом, новая машина, это платье, эти цветы, новое пальто, её глаза, его велосипед)?
2. **Decline in singular and where possible in plural:** Нет, Саша не знает (американец, женщина, урок биологии, русский язык, ваша сестра, этот человек, эта опера, французская история)
3. **Combine quantitative words with nouns:** Сегодня у нас (было / будет) много, мало, больше, меньше, нет (вино, вода, водка, гость, кофе, лекция, лодка, мясо, нож, стакан)
Supply the correct forms: 1. Машина (господин Кузнецов). 2. Машина (госпожа Кузнецова). 3. Город (Ленинград). 4. Сейчас у меня урок (пение, математика, химия). 5. Котёл (горячая вода). 6. Сколько у вас (сын, дочь, ребёнок, брат, сестра, друг)? 7. Сколько вам (год)? 8. Больше (суп, студент, человек, песок). 9. Она не слушает (музыка, радио, урок). 10. В этом районе нет (дождь, облака, яблоки, кино, болезнь, горы).

Translate: 1. You're looking at Svetlov's store. 2. I didn't see the bus. 3. Sonya doesn't like her mother. 4. What color is your new car? 5. Barbara was late for her Russian lesson. 6. There's plenty of sugar on the table. 7. She buys cheese every day. 8. Boris is a student at the University of Oxford. 9. There were no beds in the room. 10. We don't have enough bread. 11. We need more paper and pencils. 12. It rains a lot here in the merry month of May.

25. GENITIVE CASE II

A. **Usage after Verbs.** Certain verbs are followed by the genitive, among them бояться, be afraid of; желать, wish (e.g. я желаю вам успеха, I wish you success; this same formula is implied in expressions such as спокойной ночи, good night; всего хорошего, good luck; счастливого пути, bon voyage); добиваться, strive for (perf. добиться, obtain, achieve); достигать (perf. достигнуть), reach, attain; касаться, touch upon, concern (e.g. это касается сестры, this concerns sister).

Another group of verbs may take either the **genitive or the accusative** with inanimate objects, depending on whether the object is definite or specific, and only the accusative with animate objects: ждать, wait for (e.g. он ждёт жену, he is waiting for his wife; он ждёт поезд, he is waiting for <u>the</u> (a specific) train; but он ждёт поезда, he is waiting for <u>a</u> (any) train); искать, look for; требовать (perf. по-), demand; спрашивать (perf. спросить), ask for (information); просить (perf. по-) ask for (a favor). Note that with these verbs "for" is often found in English, but do <u>not</u> translate this into

Russian with a preposition such as для or за. Compare
also the usage of the genitive with verbs such as дать,
хотёть, купи́ть (above, 24B).

B. Usage with Prepositions. The genitive is governed by
the most prepositions of any case. Primary prepositions
include: у, by, near; at (one's home or place of business); in one's possession (used in "have" constructions,
e.g. у меня́ маши́на, I have a car; до, up to, as far as;
until, before; с (со), off, down from; since; от, away
from; from (a person); из, out of, from; без, without;
для, for (the sake, purpose, benefit of).

Note that из is the opposite of в, and с likewise the
opposite of на wherever it would be used, e.g., в го́род,
into the city; из го́рода, out of the city; на заво́д, на
рабо́ту, to the factory, to work; с заво́да, с рабо́ты, from
the factory, from work. An exception: в посте́ль, into
bed, but с посте́ли, out of bed. With people, the proper
prepositions are: к, to (with the dative); у, at; от, from.

The great majority of secondary prepositions (i.e., those
derived from other parts of speech) take the genitive.
The most common are вме́сто, instead of; вне, outside;
внутри́, inside; во вре́мя, during; во́зле, alongside; во-
кру́г, around; вро́де, like, resembling; из-за, from behind;
on account of; из-под, from under; кро́ме, besides, except;
ми́мо, by, past; насчёт, about, concerning; о́коло, near,
around; approximately; по́сле, after; про́тив, opposite;
against; среди́, in the midst of, among.

Exercises. Oral Drills. 1. Combine verbs with objects:
Ва́ня ждал, и́щет, спроси́л, тре́бует (авто́бус, э́тот авто́бус,
кни́ги, кни́ги кото́рые он вам одолжи́л, объясне́ние, сове́т,
Та́ня, ма́льчик)
2. Decline nouns with their proper prepositions: (a) Мы
пришли́ в / к / на (банк, библиоте́ка, вокза́л, го́род, Ива́н,
конто́ра, конце́рт, рабо́та, сестра́, учи́тель) (b) Repeat
with мы бы́ли в, на, у... and (c) with мы ушли́ из, от, с...

Translate: 1. What are you afraid of? 2. Donna is afraid
of dogs. 3. What are you looking for? 4. I'm looking for
my sister. 5. Sonya is waiting for a bus. 6. He's waiting for a taxi. 7. I'm waiting for a rainy day. 8. Why
did you say "best of luck" instead of "good night"? 9.
The teacher requires a paper every week. 10. One of my
friends is living with us. 11. We can listen to the radio
at Ivan's place. 12. I'm doing this for my father. 13.
I paid ten rubles for this gift. 14. Steven got a letter
from Moscow. 15. Tanya got a letter from her uncle. 16.
He has about a hundred books. 17. She had big eyes and
long hair. 18. We went from the meeting to the theater,
and after the theater we took Smith to the station. Then
we came home from the station. 19. I'm bored without you.
20. Did that happen before the war? No, it happened during

the war. 21. They'll be here until Friday. 22. Nina is
making a drawer out of metal. 23. They walked around the
lake. 24. The bank is opposite the hotel. 25. They are
not playing because of the rain. 26. Tolstoy lived among
peasants. 27. When he got into bed, his wife got out of
bed. 28. I want nothing except a new hat. 29. For a
long time we strove for good results but achieved nothing.
30. How about my car?

26. DATIVE CASE

A. **Indirect Object.** The recipient, usually a person, of
the action of verbs having to do with giving, saying,
showing, sending, writing, etc., is in the dative, where-
as the thing given, shown, etc., is in the accusative,
being the direct object, e.g. он показа́л мне кни́гу, he
showed me the book. When the indirect object follows
rather than precedes the direct in English, "to" must be
used: "He showed the book to me." But the preposition is
not to be translated into Russian here: *он показа́л кни́гу
ко мне is wrong. The "to" idea is also seen in expressions such as приве́т друзья́м, greetings to friends;
ра́дость ма́тери, a joy to mother; коне́ц сме́ху, an end to
laughter, etc. However, "to" may also be rendered in
Russian by various prepositions, depending on context
(see D below).

B. **Other Verbs.** Certain verbs, in which the idea of
"giving to" is less apparent than in the above, have a
personal object in the dative rather than the accusative:
ве́рить, believe (я ве́рю вам, I believe you, but note я
ве́рю в вас, I believe _in_ you); звони́ть, call, phone;
меша́ть, disturb, hinder; обеща́ть, promise; отвеча́ть,
answer (он отвеча́ет мне, he answers me, but он отвеча́ет
на вопро́с, he answers the question); помога́ть, help;
сле́довать, follow; сове́товать, advise. A special case is
the verb учи́ть, teach, and its reflexive form учи́ться
learn, study. The person taught is in the accusative,
and the subject taught or studied in the dative, the opposite of English usage: он у́чит Ни́ну му́зыке, he is teaching Nina music; Ни́на у́чится му́зыке, Nina is studying music.

C. For the usage of the dative in **impersonal expressions**,
see Sections 52-53.

D. **Prepositions.** The only primary prepositions which take
the dative are к (ко before мне, всем, etc.) and по. The
former indicates motion **toward** a thing or place (where
в means "to, into") or **to** a person. Thus, "to the theater"
is в теа́тр, not к теа́тру, which would mean "toward the
theater building"; and "to Ivan" is к Ива́ну, not в Ива́на,
which would mean "into Ivan." Note again that к is not
used after verbs of giving, saying, etc. The preposition
по has various meanings: along, over the surface of (по

у́лице, along the street; по го́роду, around town); over,
on (по телефо́ну, over the phone; по телеви́зору, on tele-
vision); by, according to (по мои́м часа́м, by my watch;
по расписа́нию, according to the schedule); note also the
idioms по мо́ему, ва́шему, etc., in my, your, etc. opinion.
Secondary prepositions taking the dative include благо-
даря́, thanks to, because of; and вопреки́, in spite of.

Exercises. Oral Drill. Decline the objects properly,
using both indirect and direct where possible:
Това́рищи, пожа́луйста, да́йте--чита́йте--пиши́те--скажи́те--
спроси́те--отве́тьте--обеща́йте--объясни́те--покажи́те--
купи́те--пригласи́те--помоги́те--позвони́те--сове́туйте--не
меша́йте--слу́шайте (я, он, она́, мы, они́, Ко́ля, Степа́нов,
наш дире́ктор, э́та де́вушка, э́ти гра́ждане) (паке́т, карти́на,
письмо́)

Supply the correct forms: 1. Не говори́те (me) об э́том.
2. Мы посла́ли (Скря́бин) и (Ба́рсова) пода́рки. 3. (На́ши
лю́ди) тру́дно понима́ть ва́ши иде́и. 4. Да́йте (him) кни́ги, а
(her) бума́гу. 5. Мы бы́стро бежа́ли по (тропи́нка) к (мо́ре).
6. Благодаря́ (э́тот вели́кий учёный), мы мо́жем слу́шать
переда́чи по (ра́дио). 7. Помоги́ (me), кри́кнул Серге́й, и я
бро́сился к (him). 8. Почему́ ты не купи́л (yourself) паль-
то́? 9. Она́ всё боле́ет, хо́дит по (doctors), но не сле́дует
их (advice). 10. У́мный студе́нт--ра́дость (учи́тель).

Translate: 1. He told me the whole story. 2. Nina is
writing a letter to Peter. 3. What did you send Pavlov?
4. Who did you send to Pavlov? 5. Let's put an end to
this silly game and go to the movies. 6. They can either
go to the club or to Nikolay's. 7. Come to me this evening, dear. 8. I advise you to call your mother right
away. 9. Fyodor wrote me he doesn't believe in God, but
I don't believe him. 10. What is George studying? Sam-
sonov is teaching him physics. 11. If you don't answer
the teacher, he will only ask you more questions. 12.
According to the evening paper, we can see it on tele-
vision. 13. Promise me you won't disturb Father. 14.
We strolled all over town, then went to the station.

27. INSTRUMENTAL CASE

A. **Basic Usage** of the instrumental is to indicate the
agency of an action, answering the question "with (by
means of) what"?: писа́ть карандашо́м, write with a pencil;
éхать по́ездом, go by train, etc. Note that **no preposition**
is used to translate the English "with" in this context
(cf. the usage of с in D below). Often, the instrumental
is **adverbial** in function, answering the question "how?",
e.g. идти́ домо́й ле́сом, go home by way of the forest;
рабо́тать инжене́ром, to work as an engineer; говори́ть
шо́потом, speak in a whisper. For the usage of the instrumental in **time expressions**, see 51B.

B. <u>Predicate Usage</u>. The English "predicate nominative"
is regularly in the instrumental in Russian when the verb
"to be" is expressed; i.e., everywhere except in the present tense: Николай бу́дет до́ктором; Николай хо́чет быть
до́ктором; Ко́ля, будь до́ктором! etc. The exception to this
is the past tense, with which, as a rule, the predicate is
in the instrumental when a temporary state is implied but
in the nominative when the state is permanent, e.g. Че́хов
был до́ктором as opposed to Че́хов был писа́тель (he prac-
ticed medicine only for a short period, but was a writer
his whole adult life). Also note situations such as кто
это был? Это был до́ктор (an irrevocable fact). When there
is doubt as to whether a state is temporary or permanent,
the usage of the instrumental is preferred in contemporary
Russian.

Other verbs of being, becoming, etc., which require a
predicate in the instrumental are явля́ться, a literary
synonym of быть in addition to its basic meaning of "appear"; станови́ться (perf. стать), become; остава́ться
(оста́ться), remain; каза́ться, seem; счита́ться, be considered. Certain non-reflexive verbs may take both a direct
object in the accusative and a complement in the instrumental, e.g. студе́нты счита́ют его́ хоро́шим учи́телем, the
students consider him a good teacher.

C. <u>Verbs and Adjectives</u>. Certain reflexive verbs in addition to those noted above have an object in the instrumental without a preposition: горди́ться, be proud of;
занима́ться, study, be occupied with; интересова́ться, be
interested in; по́льзоваться, use, make use of; among
others. Verbs of directing, governing, etc., regularly
take the instrumental, e.g., владе́ть, own, possess, be
master of; пра́вить, govern, drive, steer; руководи́ть, lead,
guide. Also note expressions involving bodily motion:
кача́ть (качну́ть) голово́й, shake one's head; кива́ть (кив-
ну́ть) голово́й nod one's head; маха́ть (махну́ть) руко́й, wave
one's hand; пожима́ть (пожа́ть) плеча́ми, shrug one's shoulders

The <u>short forms</u> of a few <u>adjectives</u> are often followed by
the instrumental: бога́тый, rich (in); дово́льный, satisfied
(with) (недово́льный, dissatisfied); за́нятый, busy, occupied
(with). But note that по́лный, full (of) is used with the
<u>genitive</u>.

D. <u>Prepositions</u>. Six prepositions take the instrumental.
С (со before мной, все́ми, etc.) in the meaning of "along
with, together with" must not be confused with the idea of
"using, by means of", in which no preposition is used:
писа́ть перо́м, <u>not</u> *писа́ть с перо́м; but идти́ с бра́том, <u>not</u>
*идти́ бра́том. Note the use of с with a plural pronoun to
link closely associated people where English uses simply
"and": мы с жено́й, my wife and I; вы с Ива́ном, you and
Ivan; or, with two nouns, де́душка с ба́бушкой, grandfather
and grandmother; likewise, with closely associated objects,

e.g. хлеб с ма́слом, bread and butter. За, behind, beyond, and под, under, take the instrumental when <u>location</u> rather than motion is indicated, e.g. мы стоя́ли за гаражо́м, we were standing behind the garage. За has additional meanings of "after", "for", e.g. они́ сле́дуют за мной, they are following (after) me; она́ пошла́ за водо́й, she went for (to get, "fetch") water. Also note the expression of a woman's marital status: Ни́на за́мужем за Серге́ем, Nina is married to Sergey. <u>But</u> за takes the accusative after a verb of motion in Ни́на вышла (выхо́дит) за́муж за Серге́я, Nina married (is marrying) Sergey. Ме́жду, between; пе́ред, before, in front of; and над, over, above, take only the instrumental, although occasionally ме́жду is found with the genitive in set expressions such as ме́жду двух огне́й, "between the devil and the deep blue sea". Note the expressions рабо́тать над, work on; смея́ться над, laugh at.

<u>Exercises</u>. Oral Drills. 1. Use every feasible combination of I, II, and III: I. Това́рищ Петро́в говори́т--горди́тся--дово́лен--е́дет--ест--за́нят--интересу́ется--пи́шет--по́льзуется--рабо́тает--смеётся--стои́т--хо́дит II. no preposition; с, за, под, пе́ред, над, ме́жду III. я, ты, он, она́, мы, вы, они́, авто́бус, ви́лка, гара́ж, гро́мкий го́лос, де́вушки, друзья́, кни́га, маши́на, меха́ник, мя́со, перо́, по́ле, ру́сский язы́к
2. Make every combination of verb with predicate:
Анто́н Па́влович Че́хов --(present tense of быть), хо́чет быть, бу́дет, был, стал, ста́нет (до́ктор, вели́кий ру́сский писа́тель, наш друг, сла́вный челове́к)

Supply the correct forms: 1. Пиши́те на доске́ то́лько (бе́лый мел). 2. Со́лнце сия́ло над (земля́). 3. Назва́ли Гри́бова (ста́рый хрен). 4. Ве́ра интересу́ется (живо́тные), а я бою́сь (them). 5. Если ты недово́лен (with me), почему́ ты идёшь (with me)? 6. Кто бу́дет руководи́ть (учрежде́ние)? 7. Мы стоя́ли под (си́льный дождь) пе́ред (ваш дом). 8. Они́ побежа́ли за (гара́ж) и на́чали смея́ться над (us).

Translate: 1. I like to travel by plane. 2. We're going by subway. 3. She opened the letter with a knife. 4. She wants to go to the movies with Peter. 5. My brother and I also want to go. 6. Sidorov nodded but Nikolaev only shrugged his shoulders. 7. Our uncle works out of town as a factory director. 8. Are you satisfied with Peter? 9. Tanya will become a physician. 10. Herman Melville was a great American writer. 11. Tolstoy was a soldier. He later became a great writer. 12. Sonya seems to be an intelligent student. 13. She considers her teacher stupid. 14. I remain your good friend. 15. That was your brother. 16. I don't know how to use this dictionary. 17. They are all studying Russian. 18. They are full of energy. 19. Who will guide us? 20. Sonya waved her hand and went to get the evening paper. 21. Tanya is marrying Victor and her sister is married to Peter. 22. Between us, Rimsky

is working on a new novel. 23. Why are you shaking your
head? 24. They put their books under the bed. 25. Do
you keep your books under the bed?

SUPPLEMENTARY TRANSLATION EXERCISE. Yesterday Peter and
I were at the movies. We saw the film A Man for All
Seasons (use "times"). I usually go to the movies to
see the stars (use the literal звезда́), not the film.
But there were no stars in this film; all the actors
were English. The movie was about Thomas More and his
wife and daughter, who lived during the reign of Henry
(Ге́нрих) VIII, King of England. After the movie we went
to the market to buy some beer, then by bus to Bill's to
drink and play cards. We always do that at Bill's. Bill
was a thief (вор) for many years, but now he's a hero to
all the kids--a fireman (пожа́рник). He tells us that as
a boy he wanted to become President of the U.S.A. I believe him. But today he's interested only in beer and
cards. Peter does better: he is studying music. And I
do even better. Although I'm studying English and French
history, French literature, and many other subjects, and
will become a French teacher, my main interest is--women.

28. ADVERBS

A. Location and Motion. The adverbs of place "where",
"here", and "there" have a double translation in Russian,
depending on whether location or motion is involved.
Compare the usage of the prepositional and accusative
cases with в and на (23). Corresponding to the question
где? where (at)? are здесь (тут), here, and там, there;
to the question куда? where (to)? are the rhyming words
сюда́, (to) here, and туда́,(to) there (cf. the archaic
English "whither", "hither", "thither"). Thus it is in-
correct to say in Russian *где вы идёте?, *я иду́ там,
etc., although these are surprisingly easy mistakes to
make. Note also отку́да? from where?, and the answering
отсю́да, from here, and отту́да, from there. The adverbs
до́ма, at home, and домо́й, (to) home, homeward, show a
similar distinction: мы сиди́м до́ма, we are staying at
home; мы идём домо́й, we are going home. Here, the answer
to отку́да is и́з дому, away from home.

B. Other Distinctions of Usage. Certain other Russian
adverbs appear to be synonymous because in English they
may be translated by the same word. Sometimes the distinction has to do merely with frequency of usage or
style, as in здесь and тут, here, of which здесь is the
more often used on various levels and тут is largely con-
fined to colloquial speech; везде́, everywhere, more often
used than the literary всю́ду; то́же, preferred to та́кже
in the meaning of (I, you, he, etc.) too, also.

In other cases there are semantic differences: only
may be used in the sense of "in addition" when only one
subject is involved, e.g. я говорю по-английски, (а)
также (и) по-русски, I speak English and also Russian.
Also note: теперь and сейчас, now. Although on occasion
the two are loosely used synonymously, теперь has the
broader meaning of "nowadays, at present," while сейчас
in its literal meaning of "this hour" refers to the immediate moment. Потом, затем and тогда, then. The first
two translate "then" in the sense of "after that," with
затем having the more immediate meaning of "next", e.g.
мы зашли к Саше, а затем к Ване, we dropped in on Sasha,
and then on Vanya; while тогда can mean "at that time"
(e.g. тогда я ещё жил в Англии, then I was still living
in England) or "in that case" (лампа вам не нравится?
Тогда не покупайте её, you don't like the lamp? Then don't
buy it). Опять, снова and ещё раз, again. Снова has the
special sense of "anew, afresh" (сделаем это снова, let's
do it over again); ещё раз of "one more time" (попробуем
ещё раз, let's try once again). Всегда and всё время,
always. When a specific action is involved, the sense of
"all the time, constantly" is better translated by всё
время, or simply всё, e.g. эта девушка всё (время)
смеётся, this girl is always laughing. For the difference
between долго and давно, for a long time, see 36A.

C. Translation of "Very Much", "Too Much". Очень много
is used in a quantitative sense: очень много книг, very
many books; он очень много пьёт, he drinks very much, etc.
With mental verbs such as любить, хотеть, бояться, etc.,
много alone expresses degree or intensity: я очень люблю
его, I like (love) him very much, not *я люблю его очень
много. (N.B. большое спасибо, thanks very much.) Много
is likewise not used with слишком in similar circumstances:
слишком много книг, пьёт, too many books, drinks too much,
etc., but слишком любит, loves too much. Слишком itself
is generally omitted in phrases like "it's too early, late
(to); you're too young (to), etc., e.g. рано думать об
этом, it's too early to think about that.

Exercises. Oral Drill: form all possible questions and
their possible answers, using both adverbs and appropriate
prepositional phrases: (Где, куда, откуда) вы были, идёте,
живёте, работаете, бежите, положили пластинки, сидели,
сели? Я (verb) здесь, там, сюда, туда, отсюда, оттуда,
дома, домой, из дому.

Translate: 1. These birds are found everywhere. 2. I
haven't seen Tom for a long time--what's he doing now?
3. Is Tom in the kitchen? What's he cooking now? 4.
Sonya was late to school today. Me too. 5. We used to
go to the opera, and then to the club. 6. Then, Semenov
was president of the club. He was also the secretary.
7. Say that again, please. 8. I don't understand that
woman, she's always crying. 9. Mister Garfinkel, I love

you very much. 10. I want to be with you very much. 11.
Jack is very much interested in trains, and he reads very
much about them. 12. Nadya thinks too much about her doctor. 13. It's too late for Smith to think about anything
--he's dead. 14. Thanks a lot for the news!

29. CONJUNCTIONS I

A. И, а, and но. The conjunction а, in the meaning of
"and" or "but", often overlaps with и and но. In general,
however, it points out a contrast and thus separates, where
и is a joining connective that can be considered the equivalent of a plus sign: Ваня и Маша работает (i.e., Ваня
работает и Маша работает), but Ваня работает, а Маша
играет. Here а can also be translated "while": John is
working,while Mary is playing. Note the characteristic
usage of а at the beginning of a sentence, introducing a
new subject: я еду в город. А вы? I'm going to the city.
And you? (How about you?) Но has a stronger adversative
meaning; it is used when "but" can be replaced with nothing weaker such as "and" or "while": он добрый, но глупый
человек, he is a kind but stupid person.

Also found in the meaning of "but, however" are однако
and the particle же: он был на собрании, однако ничего
не сказал, he was at the meeting, but (however) said
nothing; он играет, я же буду работать, he is playing,
but I (on the other hand) will work. (The conjunction
а could be used here as well.) Note that же, as an unstressed enclitic, has a fixed position as the second
word in the clause; i.e., it appears after the subject
of that clause. The conjunction и has the additional
meanings of "also", "even": она не только красивая женщина, но и добрая, she is not only a beautiful but also
a kind woman; это необычно и для него, that's unusual
even for him. Даже also renders "even"; note that "not
even" is даже не: он даже не хотел воды, he didn't even
want water.

B. Distributive Conjunctions. These include: и...и, both
...and: она и красивая и добрая, she is both beautiful and
kind; или...или, either...or: Ваня работает или в конторе
или дома, Vanya is working either at the office or at home;
ни...ни, neither...nor (or either...or with negated verb):
дети не играют ни на лугу ни в лесу, the children are not
playing either in the meadow or in the forest; то...то,
now...now: птица появилась то тут, то там, the bird ap-
peared now here, now there. "Or else" is а то or (а) не
то: поспешите, (а) не то вы опоздаете, Hurry or else
you'll be late.

C. Subordinating Conjunctions. Among the most important
are: чтобы, in order to, in order that (see 43C); потому
что, because, and the closely related так как, since (e.g.

я ничего не мог купить, так как у меня не было денег,
I couldn't buy anything because I had no money); если,
if (если...то, if...then, see 42); ли, whether, if (follows the word carrying logical stress in a subordinate
clause: не знаю, дома ли он, I don't know if (whether)
he is home. Note that as an <u>interrogative</u> particle, ли
has no translation and is seldom used in the spoken
language: знает ли он урок? Does he know the lesson?);
пока, while, during the time that (e.g. шёл дождь пока
мы играли, while we were playing it rained; also note
пока...не, until: я ждал, пока банк не открылся, I waited
until the bank opened); едва, hardly, barely; хотя, although; несмотря на, in spite of (followed by accusative;
cf. смотреть на). Note that these conjunctions, except
for the particle ли, are always preceded by commas.

D. For the usage of conjunctions in <u>comparison</u>, see 47;
in <u>conditional expressions</u>, see 42-43.

<u>Exercises</u>. Translate: 1. Sergey is reading and Kolya is
writing. 2. Vanya is playing the piano and singing songs.
3. I'm working in a store now. And what is Rose doing?
4. This isn't a house, but a hotel. 5. I live with Sokolov, but I don't like him. 6. I don't like him because
he is neither intelligent nor kind. 7. Liza is German
while Tamara is Russian. 8. Stepan not only doesn't know
his lesson, but he never comes to class either. 9. Father
was ill; however, Vanya continued to play the piano. 10.
Sonya did not even know Father was ill. 11. I told Vanya
to stop, since Father was ill, or else I would beat him.
12. In spite of my threat (угроза) Vanya now smiled, now
laughed at me. 13. He was either angry at me or at Father.
14. I didn't know whether Father had beaten him. 15. But
he said he would play until Father got out of bed. 16.
Although he was ill, Father got up in order to beat Vanya.
17. He had hardly opened his door when Vanya ran out of
the house.

30. CONJUNCTIONS II

A. <u>Subordinate clauses introduced by что, как, когда.</u>
In English, the conjunction "that" is frequently omitted:
he said (that) he was coming; I expect him to come (i.e.,
I expect that he will come), etc. But such is not the
case in Russian; что must be expressed and preceded by a
comma: он сказал, что он придёт; я ожидаю, что он придёт,
etc. Note also how sentences such as "we watched them
playing," "we listened to her sing," etc., are rendered
in Russian: мы смотрели, как они играли; мы слушали,
когда она пела (literally, "we saw <u>how</u> they played, we
listened <u>when</u> she was singing,"etc.)

B. <u>Prepositions extended into conjunctive phrases</u>. In English, words such as "before" and "after" serve both as prepositions before noun phrases and conjunctions before verbal phrases, e.g. "this happened after the meeting"; "this happened after he went home." But in Russian, a distinction is necessary: это случилось после собрания, but это случилось после того, как он пошёл домой. Likewise: дети моют руки перед обедом, the children wash their hands before dinner, but дети вымыли руки перед тем, как обедали, the children washed their hands before eating dinner. Compare also the preposition до, before, until, with до того, как and с, since, with с тех пор, как in similar usages, e.g. с тех пор, как я переехал сюда, since (lit. since those times that) I moved here...

C. <u>Sentences balanced by то or definite adverb</u>. In English it is possible to follow a preposition immediately with an adverb or conjunction, e.g. "he thought about how his father died"; "that depends on whether he comes." As this is not possible in Russian, since a preposition must be followed by something declinable, the sentence is "balanced" by a form of the demonstrative pronoun то, "that": он думал о том, как умер отец; это зависит от того, придёт ли он.

The stressed relative pronoun что (English "what" in the sense of "that which") is also preceded by a form of то, which, however, may be omitted in the accusative, or the genitive after a negated verb: я знаю (то), что он делает; я не знаю (того), что он делает, I know (don't know) what he is doing; мы боимся того (гордимся тем, думаем о том, etc.), что он делает we are afraid of (proud of, thinking about, etc.) what he is doing.

Note also the use of balancing adverbs in sentences like эти цветы растут только там, где дождь идёт, these flowers grow only where it rains; поеду туда, куда и брат, I'll go where my brother goes; они играют даже тогда, когда темно, they play even when it is dark.

<u>Exercises</u>. Translate: 1. I think he's a very good teacher. 2. I often think about what he says in class. 3. Do you understand what he is saying? 4. No, but I am interested in what he is saying. 5. We heard you were ill. 6. We heard Tanya sing Russian songs. 7. Excuse me for being late. 8. They're still waiting for him to come. 9. Semyon went to Moscow after his father died. 10. Semyon always went to the movies after supper. 11. Get dressed before Father sees you. 12. I have been working since early morning. 13. I have been working since I came home. 14. Have you thought about whether Svetlov will come? 15. Vanka played the piano even when his father was ill. 16. He ran to where his father could not run. 17. I saw him run into the woods myself.

31. PERSONAL PRONOUNS

Review the declension of personal pronouns in the Appendix, noting especially that the forms of он, она, оно, and они take a prefixed н- after prepositions, e.g. ему, but к нему.

A. <u>Distinction between ты and вы</u>. The singular ты is used in addressing relatives, friends, children, animals, and divine beings; in other contexts, it has the effect of an insult. It corresponds to the archaic English "thou". The plural вы is used in polite or formal situations, e.g. in addressing superiors, strangers, or mere acquaintances. It is capitalized when addressing such a person in writing. It must also be used, of course, to address more than one person, and is always used with the plural form of the verb and <u>short</u> adjective (not the long form, which is singular if only one person is addressed): вы правы, but вы русский (русская).

B. <u>Omission</u>. The answer to a question in Russian may be a mere repetition of the word that carries the logical stress, without a pronoun and with or without да: ты хочешь кофе? -(Да), хочу, do you want coffee? --Yes, I do; она милая девушка? -Милая, is she a nice girl? --Yes, she is. A negative answer would add the negative particle: (нет), не хочу.

The omission of the pronoun in the third person plural renders an <u>impersonal</u> meaning: говорят, что он злой человек, they (i.e., people in general; the English "they" has no definite antecedent here) say he is a wicked man; здесь таких книг не читают, such books aren't read here (lit. "here they don't read such books"). The second person singular without pronoun conveys the impersonal "you", e.g. ничего не поделаешь, you can't do anything, there is nothing to be done.

C. <u>Translation of "it"</u>. When the antecedent of "it" is a specific thing, the translation is он, она, or оно, depending on the gender of the noun: это стол. <u>Он</u> мой. Это моя комната. <u>Она</u> красива. Видишь окно? Открой <u>его</u>. But when "it" refers to an abstract idea or something not definitely expressed in an antecedent, the proper translation is это, e.g. это было интересное событие, it was an interesting event; кто это? who is it?; не говорите об этом, don't talk about it. "It" is <u>not</u> translated at all in sentences like "it was winter"; "it is cold"; etc., where the "it" is completely impersonal and indefinite: была зима; холодно.

D. <u>The Reflexive Pronoun себя</u> always refers back to the subject, and has no plural forms: он видит себя, они видят себя в зеркале, he sees himself, they see themselves in the mirror. Note that in many cases this reflexive

idea becomes -ся (-сь), attached to the verb: он одевáет-
ся, мóется, etc., he dresses himself, washes himself,
etc. <u>But</u> он чýвствует себя хорошó, he feels well; он
ведёт себя плóхо, he behaves poorly. Себя is obligatory
if the personal object is the same as the subject: вы
не знáете <u>себя</u>, not *вас; я говорил с ним о <u>себé</u>, not
*обо мне.

<u>Exercises</u>. Oral drill: combine the verbs and prepositions
with the proper forms of the pronouns:
Кузнецóвы приезжáют в гóрод (встрéтить, без, помогáть, к,
и горди́тся, с, и дýмают о) (я, ты, он, онá, мы, вы, они́)

Supply the correct forms: 1. Мы пошли́ (with him). 2. Он
танцевáл (with me) а потóм (with her). 3. Вы довóльны
(with them)? 4. Я недовóлен (with myself). 5. Я никогдá
не дýмаю (about them). 6. Я дýмаю тóлько (about myself).
7. Не знáю, дýмает ли онá (about me). 8. Это извéстная
кни́га: вы никогдá не слы́шали (about it)? 9. Я скучáю
(without you). 10. Он купи́л (her) ю́бку, а (himself) ру-
бáшку. 11. Вот перó. Ви́дишь (it)? 12. Не серди́тесь так
(at us). 13. Посмотри́те (at me)! 14. Где рýчка? Я не
ви́жу (it). 15. Сегóдня вéчером мы зайдём (to you), а за-
тéм (to him). 16. Они́ побежáли (after her). 17. Это
тóлько (between us). 18. Вот письмó (from them). 19. Иди́
(with me). 20. Я возьмý (you) в кинó (with me). 21. Возь-
ми́те (with you) перó.

Translate: Are you a scientist, Mr. Pavlov? 2. You're
right, little boy. 3. What did you say, Uncle? 4. Are
you going, Sasha? --Yes, I am. 5. In the office they
said he was at home. 6. They say he never drinks. 7.
In this country you always eat too much, you don't know
what else to do. 8. My wife and I went to the market.
9. Do you think it's too hot here? 10. I don't know, I
never thought about it. 11. It's a pencil, not a pen.
12. It's me, Sasha. 13. It was September when Father
returned. 14. Get dressed and behave yourself. 15. How
do you feel, my friends? 16. He was talking about himself, not me.

32. POSSESSIVE PRONOUNS

A. <u>Usage</u>. The possessives мой, твой, свой, наш, and ваш
correspond in gender, number and case to the thing possessed, <u>not</u> the possessor: Ивáн читáет свою́ кни́гу, not
*свой кни́гу. They are thus treated as adjectives. Remem-
ber that твой corresponds to ты and ваш to вы in usage.
Review the declensions in the Appendix. For the third
person there are no special forms; the genitive personal
pronouns егó, её, and их are used, and as such are indeclinable. In contrast to the personal pronouns, they
<u>do not</u> take н- after a preposition: у негó, he has, but

у его брата, his brother has; я думаю о ней, I'm thinking
about her, but я думаю о её сестре, I'm thinking about
her sister, etc. Not without good reason, many grammarians consider the lack of regular third person possessives
a weakness in Russian.

B. The Reflexive свой may replace мой, твой, etc., in the
first and second persons, emphasizing the idea of "one's
own." It is obligatory in the third person when the subject is the possessor, to avoid ambiguity: Сергей смотрит
на свою лошадь, Sergey is looking at his (own) horse.
Сергей смотрит на его лошадь would mean that Sergey is
looking at someone else's horse. But note that свой can
refer only to the subject of its own clause; it cannot be
the subject in a subordinate clause: он хорошо знает
свою жену, but он знает, что его жена больна, he knows
that his wife is ill (only the context could resolve any
possible ambiguity here as to whose wife it is). It can
be the grammatical subject only in certain possessive or
dative phrases, e.g. у них свой дом, they have their own
house; мне нужна своя машина, I need my own car. The
adjective собственный, one's own, could also be used here,
and is the only possibility in other contexts, e.g., это
моя собственная машина, this is my own car. Note also
certain idiomatic uses of свой: я сам не свой, I'm not
myself; между нами он свой человек, he's one of us. The
plural свои means "one's people, folks."

C. Omission. If no special emphasis is desired, the possessives are normally omitted when the subject is the
possessor, or when it is otherwise clear from the context
who is the possessor. This is especially the case with
relatives, parts of the body, and articles of clothing,
e.g. я видел брата на собрании, I saw (my) brother at the
meeting; почему закрываешь глаза, why do you close (your)
eyes?; он снял шляпа, he took off (his) hat.

In certain expressions involving parts of the body, personal pronouns are found instead of possessives. Note
the following typical examples: он пожал мне руку, he
shook my hand (rather than *он пожал мою руку); пришло
мне в голову, it came into my head (i.e., occurred to me);
она сломала себе ногу, she broke her leg; слёзы текли у
них из глаз, tears flowed from their eyes. Also note
Иван у себя в комнате, Ivan is in his room (rather than
Иван в своей комнате) and the omission of any noun indicating place of dwelling in придите ко мне, come to my
place; он пригласил нас к себе he invited us to his home.

Exercises. Oral drill: decline the combinations of pronoun with noun in singular and plural: Почему Даша/Даше
не: нравится/нравятся--смотрит на--осматривает--привыкла
к--интересуется--говорит о (мой, твой, его, ее, свой,
наш, ваш, их) (нож, ружьё, картина)?

Supply the correct forms: 1. Где (your) словáрь? 2. У меня нет (own) словаря; я пóльзуюсь (his). 3. Кáжется, что я потеря́л (your) ру́чку. 4. Пожáлуйста, верни́те мне (my) пласти́нку. 5. Мы ненави́дим (our) учи́телей и (their) ку́рсы. 6. Сегóдня вéчером мы зайдём к (your) дóчери. 7. Пётр крéпко поцеловáл (his) дочь и (her) ребёнка. 8. У негó есть (his own) карандаши́. 9. Мы дóлго говори́ли о (him) и (his) путешéствиях. 10. Потóм мы говори́ли о (you), господи́н Набóков, и о (your) ромáнах. 11. Ни́на не дýмает, что (her) сестрá придёт. 12. Они́ сломáют (their) гóлову! 13. Емý прия́тно весели́ться с (my) друзья́ми. 14. Я пóльзуюсь (your) топорóм, а ты пóльзуешься (mine). 15. Э́то (our) кóмната, а та (theirs).

Translate: 1. Stepanov and his wife live in our house. 2. Among us, Stepanov is like one of the family. 3. Yesterday I talked to him for a long time, then I talked to his wife. 4. I wonder if Stepanov knows I love his wife. 5. I certainly know he loves mine. 6. It looks like they need their own house. 7. Yesterday he beat his wife, and she almost broke her arm when she threw a plate at him. 8. I hope he's learned his lesson well. 9. That's why you see sorrow in his eyes so often, and why he shakes his head. 10. You see, he told me his wife doesn't care for him. 11. When I meet his wife on the street, she says, "Come to my room this evening." 12. But when I knock on the door she's never in. 13. Yesterday I saw her going into her office. 14. She has her own office, you know. 15. And that's my own office, across the street from hers. 16. "Let's meet after work," I said. 17. "Where?" she said. "My place or yours?" 18. "If you want to argue," I said, "forget about it!"

33. INTERROGATIVE-RELATIVE PRONOUNS

Review the declensions of кто, who; что, what; and чей, whose, in the Appendix; others are declined like regular adjectives.

A. Кто and что are followed by a singular verb form, кто with the masculine in the past, even if a feminine subject is obviously referred to, and что with the neuter: кто потеря́л су́мочку? who lost (her) purse?; что случи́лось? what happened? Кто may be used with a plural verb only with a plural pronoun antecedent (see the example in C below). Colloquially, что may also mean "why?" in place of почемý, e.g. что молчи́шь? why are you silent? (The perceptive student will note that почемý is made up of a preposition plus the dative case of что; compare also зачéм, for what purpose.

B. Other Translations of "What". There is a distinction between "what kind of," rendered by какóй, and "what

(which) one," rendered by кото́рый, e.g. каку́ю кни́гу вы
чита́ете? what (sort of) book are you reading?, but
кото́рую кни́гу вы чита́ете Which book (i.e., which particular one of a general series) are you reading? However,
when this distinction is not absolutely necessary, како́й
is colloquially preferred to кото́рый, just as in English
"what" also tends to cover the meaning of "which".

In certain cases "what" is translated by как, literally
"how": как? what? (when one did not hear something and
wants it repeated); как ва́ша фами́лия? What is your (last)
name?; как вы ду́маете? what do you think? (but note, when
something in particular is mentioned: что вы ду́маете об
Ива́не? what do you think about Ivan?). The exclamatory
"what" is како́й or что за (see 21C): кака́я пого́да! what
weather! Note that when an explanation or definition is
required, кто and что may be reinforced with тако́й: кто
э́то тако́й? who is this?; что э́то тако́е? what is this?

C. Relatives. Кото́рый, who, which, introduces relative
clauses and agrees in gender and number with its antecedent, but in case with its usage within the clause, e.g.
вы зна́ете челове́ка, кото́рому я дал кни́гу? do you know the
man to whom I gave the book? The relative pronoun cannot
be omitted, as is often done in English: "the book I read"
must be rendered кни́га, кото́рую я прочита́л. Note that its
position in the clause is second if a possessive genitive
is required: челове́к, мать кото́рого умерла́, the man whose
mother died. An alternative way of translating such a
phrase is челове́к, чья мать умерла́. Кто and что are used
as relatives if the antecedent is a pronoun, e.g. те из
вас, кто чита́ли кни́гу, those of you who read the book;
я вам скажу́ всё, что я зна́ю, I'll tell you all (that) I
know.

Exercises. Oral drills. 1. Use proper forms of both
кто and что where possible, with and without prepositions:
(Кто, что) вы бои́тесь--э́то де́лаете--дово́льны--ду́маете--
е́дете--жена́ты--живёте--за́мужем--вы́шли за́муж--зна́ете--
игра́ете--ку́пите пода́рок--смеётесь--хоти́те?
2. Decline in singular and plural, supplying a preposition
where necessary: Вот челове́к / же́нщина (кото́рый) живёт/
живу́т в Москве́--я люблю́--мы помога́ем--мы игра́ли в ка́рты--
я чита́л в газе́те.
Supply the correct forms: 1. (With whom) вы идёте? 2.
(With whom) вы говори́те? 3. (With whom) вы дово́льны?
4. (To whom) она́ пое́дет? 5. (To whom) она́ написа́ла?
6. (What) они́ де́лают? 7. (What) он бои́тся? 8. (Who)
идёт? 9. (Who) вы ви́дите? 10. На (who) вы смо́трите?
11. (who) ты помога́ешь? 12. (What) они́ по́льзуются?
13. (Whose) э́то ру́чка? 14. (Whose) э́то зда́ние? 15. В
(whose) до́ме вы живёте? 16. О (whose) карти́нах идёт
речь? 17. О (what) карти́не идёт речь? 18. О (which)
из э́тих карти́н идёт речь? 19. (At whose place) он

живёт? 20. О (what) де́вочка всё вре́мя ду́мает? Я не зна́ю
о (what), но зна́ю о (whom). 21. (With what) мы разру́бим
э́ту до́ску? 22. Вы зна́ете челове́ка, (who) там живёт? 23.
Вот челове́к, (whom) я уби́л. 24.Тот, (who) не ест, не живёт.
Translate: 1. Who was here? 2. What was in this box?
3. Why are you crying, Tanechka? 4. Which of you girls
was there? 5. What flowers do you like? 6. What a stupid man! 7. What do you think? 8. What are you thinking
about? 9. What's Sonya's last name? 10. What's that?
--I said, what bird is that? 11. Whose door did you open?
12. I don't know the man who called you. 13. Do you know
who took my book? 14. Do you know whose book I'm using?
15. She didn't see the man you were talking to. 16. In
a war you don't know the men you kill. 17. Whoever
doesn't work around here doesn't eat. 18. He who laughs
last laughs best.

34. DEMONSTRATIVE AND DEFINITE PRONOUNS

Review the declensions of э́тот, тот, весь, and сам in
the Appendix.

A. Demonstratives. Э́тот and тот have as literal equivalents the English "this" and "that," but in practice э́тот
generally covers the meaning of both. Тот is used, however, when a contrast is necessary, e.g. э́ти ве́щи мои́,
а те ва́ши these things are mine, and those are yours.
The abstract "that" is translated by э́то: я не ду́мал об
э́том, I didn't think about that (cf. 31C).

The impersonal form э́то is also used to mean "this is,
that is, these are, those are": э́тот каранда́ш, this pencil, but э́то каранда́ш, this is a pencil; та кни́га, that
book, but э́то кни́га, that is a book; э́ти кни́ги, these
books, but э́то кни́ги, these are books, etc. N.B. that
the emphatic "this, that is" (in the sense of "here, there
is," as in pointing) is rendered by вот, e.g. вот Ива́н,
this (here) is Ivan; вот почему́ я не пошёл, that's why I
didn't go.

The pronoun тот, in addition to its basic meaning of
"that", has several particular uses. Note the following:
на той стороне́ у́лицы, on the other side of the street;
вы взя́ли не ту кни́гу, you took the wrong book; он не то
сказа́л, he said the wrong thing; тот же (са́мый) челове́к,
та же (са́мая) же́нщина, the same man, woman (where са́мый
is used for emphasis); тот, кто, he or the one who;
возьми́те и́ли тот и́ли друго́й стул, take either chair
(either one or the other). Remember that the forms of
тот are also used in balancing sentences, where they are
not translated into English (30C).

50

B. Definite (or Determinate) Pronouns. Весь, all, whole, entire, in its neuter singular form всё means "everything", and in its plural form все, "everyone", when used alone. N.B. that in Russian the plural form of the verb must be used after the latter, e.g. все зна́ют, where we say "everybody knows." Всё is often used adverbially to mean "always, all the time" (as a shortened form of всё вре́мя; see 28B. The genitive всего́ may translate "altogether, in sum, only":у неё всего́ три кни́ги she has three books in all. Colloquially, всего́ has the meaning of "so long."

Сам, which translates the emphatic "myself, yourself, himself, themselves," etc., follows a pronoun but precedes a noun when not in the nominative, e.g. она́ сама́ э́то сде́лала, she did it herself; президе́нт сам был здесь, the president himself was here; я уви́дел самого́ президе́нта, I saw the president himself. It must not be confused with себя́, the reflexive "oneself" which serves gramatically as the object of a sentence: compare я зна́ю себя́, I know myself, with я сам зна́ю, I myself know. On the other hand, it should not be confused with са́мый, which means "the same," "the very" (see A above) or forms superlatives (48A). It is used with inanimate nouns in the sense of "right in, on, to," etc., e.g. в са́мом це́нтре го́рода, in the very (right in the) center of the city. Са́мый, in contrast to сам, is declined like a regular hard adjective.

Оди́н has pronominal usages in addition to its numerical meaning of "one": он живёт оди́н, она́ живёт одна́, мы живём одни́, he, she lives, we live alone; мо́жно купи́ть э́то в одно́м магази́не, you can buy that in a certain store; одни́ пи́шут карандашо́м, а други́е перо́м, some write with a pencil, and others with a pen; Па́вел и Григо́рий живу́т в одно́м до́ме, Pavel and Grigory live in the same house (here synonymous with в том же са́мом до́ме. Note also the idioms одни́м сло́вом, in a word, in short; одну́ мину́тку, just a minute! In certain contexts, note that "one" is not translated, e.g. у вас ста́рая маши́на, а у меня́ но́вая, you have an old car, but I have a new one.

Тако́й translates "such" in conjunction with a long adjective or noun: она́ така́я у́мная, she is such a smart one. But note the usage of так with short forms: она́ так умна́, she is so smart. (Cf. кака́я она́ у́мная, what a smart one she is; как она́ умна́, how smart she is.)

Друг дру́га, each other, one another, is declined only in its second element, like the noun друг in the singular, e.g. они́ пи́шут друг дру́гу, they write to each other. When a preposition is used, it splits the two elements: они́ говори́ли друг с дру́гом, they talked with each other.

Exercises. Oral drills. 1. Decline pronouns and nouns in singular and plural: Наш реда́ктор/на́шему реда́ктору нра́вится/нра́вятся--прочита́л--не прочита́л--обраща́ется к--

2. **Decline in singular and plural:** Мы/нас интересовал/
интересовали--осмотрели--осмотрели картины--ходили по--
интересовались--жили в (тот же самый) (город, здание,
комната) как и вы/вас.

3. **Decline:** Ваня и Маша часто боятся--встречают--говорят
о--недовольны--обращаются к--помогают--раздеваются при--
смеются над--смотрят на--ходят с (друг друга)

Supply the correct forms: 1. Продайте (these) книги, а не
(those). 2. Мы играем в (that) саду. 3. Ангелы живут на
(the other) свете. 4. Я работаю (all) день, а она работает (all) неделю. 5. Кажется, что ветер дует со (all)
сторон. 6. Мы смотрели на (herself) королёву. 7. Я только
что говорил с (the same) женщиной. 8. Мы ездили по (a
certain) шоссе около Лондона. 9. Я никогда не знал (such)
человека. 10. Почему они ненавидят (each other)? 11. Я
не верю (him), кто говорит (everyone) о (himself).
12. Маша (alone) говорит (about that).

Translate: 1. In Peter's office people are always talking about each other. 2. They talk about everything and
everybody. 3. Peter sometimes thinks about the office
where he worked last year. 4. But that office is on the
other side of the river. 5. Here is Martha, the secretary, who works in the same room. 6. "Are those your
books?" she asks. 7. "These books are mine, and those
are Henry's," answers Peter. 8. "But I read one book or
the other. 9. That's what happens when everybody works
in the same office. 10. I'm always using the wrong book,
picking up the wrong pen, looking in the wrong desk."
11. "I know that myself," says Martha. "You're such an
idiot." 12. She walks away, all (in) smiles. 13. She's
so nice, thinks Peter. 14. But he will never tell Martha
herself that. 15. That's a man for you.

35. INDEFINITE AND NEGATIVE PRONOUNS AND ADVERBS

A. <u>Indefinite Words</u>. The indefinite suffixes -то and
-нибудь are attached to interrogative pronouns and adverbs: кто-то, someone; что-нибудь, something, anything;
какой-то, some kind of; где-то, somewhere; когда-нибудь,
sometime; etc. These suffixes are unstressed and indeclinable, while the pronouns are declined as usual, e.g.
о чём-то, about something.

The suffix -то is the more definite of the two, implying
that the speaker is certain of the existence of something
or has something fairly definite in mind, although he cannot identify it more exactly. The difficulty is that
-нибудь can also be translated by "some-" when we mean
"any-": кто-нибудь пришёл? did someone (anyone) come?
(The speaker does not know whether anyone at all came.)

Да, кто́-то пришёл, yes, someone came. (The speaker knows someone came, but cannot identify him.) In practice, -то is generally found in declarative statements of the past or present tense; -нибудь in questions, imperatives, and the more indefinite or vague future: он дал (даёт) мне что́-то, but он даёт мне что́-нибудь?, да́йте мне что́-нибудь, мо́жет быть он даст мне что́-нибудь.

There are other indefinite particles. The prefixal ко́е- is nearly synonymous with -то, but ко́е-кто́ may have the special meaning of "a few, some people"; ко́е-что,"a thing or two". The suffix -либо, found in written or more formal contexts, is nearly synonymous with -нибудь, although it is considered more indefinite, implying "anyone, anything, etc., at all," e.g. да́йте э́ту кни́гу кому́-либо, give this book to anyone you like. For the usage of the still more indefinite ни (бы...ни), "whoever, whatever (might)", see 43B.

The particles are <u>not used</u> when "something, someone," etc. (in the sense of "there is something, someone, etc.) is followed by an infinitive, e.g. вам есть что де́лать? do you have something to do?; вам есть куда́ идти́? do you have somewhere to go? Compare the negatives in не́- below.

Note other translations of "some": я осмотре́л <u>не́сколько</u> карти́н, и <u>не́которые</u> мне понра́вились, I looked at some (i.e., a few, several) pictures, and some (i.e., certain ones) I liked; у вас есть хлеб? Да́йте мне <u>немно́го</u> (or, more colloquially, <u>немно́жко</u>), do you have bread? Give me some (a little). When the noun is mentioned, "some" is usually rendered by the genitive without other translation, e.g. да́йте мне хле́ба, give me some bread (see 24B). For the use of оди́н in translating "some, a certain," see 34B.

B. <u>Negative Words</u>. The prefix ни-, when attached to the same pronouns and adverbs which had -то or -нибудь above, gives the opposite meaning: никто́, nobody; ничто́ (ничего́), nothing; нигде́, nowhere, etc. The particle не always appears before the verb, after the other negative words in the sentence (the "double negative," in contrast to English, which can have only one negative element in a sentence), e.g. мы никогда́ ничего́ не де́лаем, we never do anything. Note: the nominative form ничто́, much less common than ничего́, is used only when a following verb takes an object without a preposition, e.g. ничто́ не беспоко́ит его́, nothing bothers him. Otherwise, e.g. ничего́ не случи́лось с ним, nothing happened to him. Ничего́ also has the idiomatic meanings "that's all right, it doesn't matter," or (with себе́) "not bad, so-so."

The stressed prefix не́- followed by an infinitive indicates "there is no...": не́кого спроси́ть, there is nobody to ask; не́чем бы́ло писа́ть, there was nothing to write

with; нам не́куда идти́, we have nowhere to go. Не́чего
has the idiomatic meaning "there's no use", e.g. не́чего
и говори́ть, что..., it goes without saying that...

When there is no infinitive, ни must be used with нет,
e.g. здесь никого́ (ничего́) нет, there is nobody (nothing)
here. Both ни and не are separated from the pronoun
when a preposition is used, making three separate elements: он ни с ке́м не говори́т, he isn't talking with anyone; ему́ не́ о чем говори́ть, he has nothing to talk about.

<u>Exercises</u>. Oral drills: 1. Use the proper forms of each
indefinite pronoun wherever possible: Това́рищ Петро́в, вы
ви́дите--бои́тесь--меша́ете--обраща́етесь к--е́дете с--
недово́льны--говори́те о (кто́-нибудь, что́-нибудь)?
Answer each question in the **affirmative**, using кто́-то or
что́-то, and then in the <u>negative</u>, using никто́ or ничего́,
taking care to use correct word-order.
2. Use the pronouns in their proper forms, with and without the given prepositions, and the adverbs where possible
with the verbs: Това́рищ Петро́ва, вам есть ((к, с) кто, (о)
что, где, куда́) говори́ть--де́лать--е́хать--жить--люби́ть--
писа́ть? Answer each question in the <u>negative</u>, using the
proper forms of не́кого, не́чего, and не́где, не́куда.

Translate: 1. Are you busy with something, Mr. Jones?
2. Yes, I'm busy with something. 3. And are you doing
something, Nick? 4. No, I'm not doing anything. I have
nothing to do. 5. Good, I have something to show you.
6. Let's go somewhere tonight. 7. But I don't want to
go anywhere. 8. Talk to me about something else. 9.
Someone called you this morning. 10. It was some girl
with some kind of long name. 11. That's all right; I'll
find out who it was somehow. 12. Why doesn't anyone ever
call me? 13. I know some girls. 14. That's something to
talk about. Do you like them? 15. I like some of them.
16. But they don't know anything. Nothing interests
them. 17. They only like candy. If I have candy, they
always say, "Give me some." 18. My trouble is, there's
nobody to talk to except you. 19. And I have nobody to
go anywhere with, not even you, because you never go anywhere with anybody. 20. I need somebody to have fun
with. Nothing ever happens around here.

SUPPLEMENTARY TRANSLATION EXERCISE. This is the story of
how Charley and Smiley quarreled with each other. These
two men knew each other well, and everybody knew them.
Charley, who worked on a farm (use фе́рма), often visited
his friend Smiley, who worked on the farm on the other
side of the road. What men they were! I saw them myself:
Charley as tall as a barn (амба́р), Smiley also some kind
of giant (гига́нт), like the barn itself, perhaps three
hundred pounds in all. Charley liked to eat something
every now and then, but Smiley ate all day and sometimes

all night; he ate everything he saw. He used to say he would eat the very moon if it came down (спуститься) to where he could hold it, and everybody believed him. This Sunday he was eating something when Charley asked if he could eat something too. I think he wanted some onion (лук) with horse-radish (хрен). Smiley said no, everything was his own and nobody else could eat anything. Besides, he got so hungry when he saw others eating. Charley laughed and said, "I have never seen such a glutton (обжора, masc.) anywhere. How can your wife live with you? It must be she's a pretty stupid one." With lightning in his eyes, Smiley said, "Well now, I don't know how you can live with your wife. She's a bear." "Your wife is a fish!" shouted Charley, and he called (назвать) Smiley himself a fat goose. "Did you call me fat?" Smiley wanted to know. "I did," said Charley. Then Smiley hit Charley's arm, and Charley hit Smiley's chest. "I'll break your head!" cried Smiley. "I'll bury you!" cried Charley. It was a terrible (страшный) moment, which none of us wants to think about, although I'm writing about it now. Soon the two old comrades were in their graves (могила). The trouble (беда) was in one thing: Charley and Smiley each loved only himself. As a certain Nikolay Gogol' once said, "It's hard to live in this world, gentlemen."

36. VERB TENSES

There are certain situations in which the Russian usage of tense is not what might be expected from the English point of view:

A. The Russian <u>present</u>, not the past, translates the English present perfect in sentences such as "I have lived (have been living) here for ten years" (and still do): я живу здесь десять лет. Я <u>жил</u> здесь десять лет would mean "I lived here for ten years (but no longer do)". In this context, note the difference between the adverbs давно and долго, both of which are translated "for a long time". But the former means "up to and including the present moment" (я давно живу здесь), while the latter refers to an action that has already run its course (я долго жил здесь).

B. There is no "sequence of tenses" in Russian. Sentences like "I thought you didn't like to read" become я думал, что вы не любите читать, as long as the action expressed in the subordinate clause is not actually limited to the past. Indirect quotes are in the same tense as the original; compare the English "she said she would read the article" with the Russian она сказала, что она прочитает статью, literally "she said she <u>will</u> read the article." Она сказала, что она прочитала статью would mean "she said she has read the article."

C. The English present becomes the Russian <u>future perfec-</u>
<u>tive</u> in sentences like "Give me the report when you finish
it": дайте мне доклад, когда вы <u>кончите</u> его; "If I see
him, I'll tell him": если я его <u>увижу</u>, я ему скажу; "We'll
go as soon as I write this letter": мы поедем, как только
я <u>напишу</u> это письмо. As in English, the present can be
used with future meaning if there is already an indication
of futurity in the sentence, as in завтра мы едем в Чик-
аго, tomorrow we're going to Chicago.

Colloquially, the future perfective is used in place of
the construction with мочь plus the infinitive, often
with the impersonal "you": не найдёшь человека в такой
толпе, you can't (lit. won't) find a man in such a crowd;
только Светлов ответит на этот вопрос, only Svetlov can
(lit. will) answer this question. It is also a mainstay
of proverbs, e.g. спасибо в карман не положишь, you can't
put thanks in your pocket; сказаного слова топором не
вырубишь, you can't chop out a spoken word with an axe.

<u>Exercises</u>. Translate: 1. I haven't seen Petrovich for a
long time. 2. But last year he told me he would write a
letter, and he did write one. 3. Petrovich has been working on a new machine for eight months now. 4. He said it
would make sandwiches faster than people could make them.
5. When he finishes it, he will show it to us. 6. We all
thought he was working on a new electric automobile. 7.
He had been working on such a car for a long time. 8.
Evidently, as soon as he thought of the sandwich machine,
he stopped (перестать) working on the automobile. 9. He's
coming here to talk about it next week. 10. As soon as I
write my article for the paper about Petrovich's new machine, I'm going to buy a new overcoat. 11. But you can't
buy anything without money. 12. Therefore, if I don't get
enough money for my article, I'll still be cold.

37. THE VERBAL ASPECTS

A. <u>Basic Differences of Usage</u>. The <u>imperfective</u> aspect
presents an action in <u>progress</u>, without reference to its
beginning or completion, or a general, repeated or habitual action. It is most often translated by the English
progressive tenses: они строят, строили, будут строить
дома, they are building, were building (used to build),
will be building houses. But N.B. that in certain statements of general or repeated action the translation may
be in the same tense as that used for the perfective:
the above examples, depending on context, could also be
translated "they build, built, will build houses" (in
general), as opposed to "<u>the</u> (particular) houses," which
would mean a Russian perfective (i.e. in past or future).

Only a simple or perfect English tense can translate the
<u>perfective</u> aspect, which indicates that a specific action

has been or will be <u>completed or terminated</u>: они постро́-
или, постро́ят дома́, they built (have, had built), will
build (will have built) the houses. Note that the perfective has no present tense, since an action cannot be
completed in the present, which has only a progressive
meaning. The endings which are like those of the present
have future meaning. It may be helpful to think of the
action of a perfective verb as limited, by being specific
and completed, while that of an imperfective is comparatively unlimited, in being general, progressive or a
matter of habit.

B. <u>Some Illustrative Examples</u>. Distinction between the
<u>process</u> and <u>result</u> of an action: Ко́лумб был сча́стлив не
тогда́, когда́ <u>откры́л</u> Аме́рику, а когда́ <u>открыва́л</u> её, Columbus
was happy not when he had discovered America, but while he
was discovering it. (This excellent illustration from
Dostoevsky's <u>The Idiot</u> is quoted by B. O. Unbegaun in his
<u>Russian Grammar</u>, Oxford, 1957, "The Notion of Aspect,"
pp. 206-209. For another good discussion of the complex
grammar of aspect, see Ward, <u>The Russian Language Today</u>
pp. 227-245.)

Distinction between <u>habitual-repeated</u> and <u>single</u> action:
Ве́ра ча́сто <u>покупа́ла</u> пода́рки в э́том магази́не, и сего́дня
она́ <u>купи́ла</u> три кни́ги, Vera often bought gifts at this
store, and today she bought three books.

Note also, between <u>attempted</u> and <u>successfully performed</u>
action: я <u>угова́ривал</u> всех купи́ть э́ту кни́гу, но <u>уговори́л</u>
то́лько сестру́, I urged everybody to buy (tried to talk
everybody into buying) this book, but persuaded only my
sister. Other common pairs used in this sense: добыва́ть-
ся, try to attain, strive for / доби́ться, attain; дока́з-
ывать, argue, contend / доказа́ть, prove; лови́ть, chase /
пойма́ть, catch; объясня́ть, try to explain / объясни́ть,
make clear.

C. <u>Expressions of Duration</u>. Many verbs can form "weak"
<u>perfectives in по-</u> with the meaning "for a while": он
прочита́л кни́гу, he read a book, but он почита́л, he read
for a while, with no indication of whether he actually
finished reading anything. Such perfectives may only be
used intransitively; i.e., they cannot take direct objects.
Note that if the exact amount of time is mentioned, the
<u>imperfective</u> is used, since it describes what was being
done over that duration, e.g. мы чита́ли всё у́тро, we read
all morning.

Note also here that only the <u>imperfective</u> infinitive can
be used after verbs such as "begin, continue, stop, get
used to," etc., since the action implies duration or gen-
erality rather than completion, e.g. мы на́чали чита́ть,
we began to read; я привы́к встава́ть ра́но I'm used to
getting up early.

D. **Imperfectives with Specialized Perfectives.** Certain verbs have no "direct" perfectives, i.e., those that retain the same meaning: among the most common are жить, live; работать, work; есть, eat; пить, drink; видеть, see; слышать, hear. Perfective forms of these verbs are somewhat specialized in meaning and (except for those in the durational по-) must take a direct object, while the imperfectives may be used transitively, e.g. он съел целый хлеб, he ate up, consumed a whole loaf of bread; они выпили бутылку вина, they drank (up) a bottle of wine; мы увидели Серёжу на углу, we saw (spotted, caught sight of) Seryozha on the corner. Otherwise: мы ели, we ate; мы пили, we drank; мы видели фильм, we saw a film, etc.

E. **Говорить and сказать.** This pair is given special consideration here because they are so often confused by the beginning student. The basic meaning of the verb говорить is "to speak, talk" in general, but since the perfective сказать, which means "to say, tell," has no imperfective form of its own, говорить must do double duty in the imperfective. Thus, in the present tense it is the only verb that can be used for either meaning: он говорит, he is talking, or he says, depending on context. The perfective поговорить, used with c and the instrumental, means "to speak, have a talk, chat with."

Exercises. Oral drills. 1. Use the proper aspect of each pair of verbs in an appropriate tense with each adverbial expression: Я вчера, долго, завтра, иногда, каждый день, обычно, сегодня вечером, только что, часто (читать/прочитать, получать/получить, покупать/купить, брать/взять, спрашивать/спросить, красть/украсть) журнал.
2. Use the proper aspect of each pair of verbs in all possible tenses with I and II: I. Мы весь день (готовить/приготовить, есть/съесть, посылать/послать, продавать/продать, укладывать/уложить) сандвичи II. Мы (the same verbs) много сандвичей.
3. Use each verb in all possible tenses with every possible object: Анна (говорить, сказать, поговорить) "до свидания", мне что-то, об Иване, по-английски, правду, со мной, хорошо.

Translate: 1. Tim reads every day. **2.** His father used to read books, but now he almost never reads anything except the newspaper. **3.** This morning Tim read for a while, ate a chocolate bar (шоколадка), then wrote a letter to his friend Ellen. **4.** While Ellen was reading this letter she drank beer and listened to the radio. **5.** Then she worked for a while. **6.** She worked for almost two hours. **7.** She wrote five lessons. **8.** They tell me that Tim and Ellen meet every day. **9.** But they didn't meet today. **10.** They will get together tomorrow. **11.** Yesterday I saw them in the yard and watched them for a while. **12.** For several minutes I watched them play. **13.** I won't tell you what they were doing. **14.** Afterward, we all had a chat about

life at the university. 15. Ellen said she didn't like
Professor Grant. 16. But Tim has always said Grant was
a good professor. 17. I used to say that too. 18. Others
tell me they don't know. 19. What do you say? 20. Please
tell me what you think. 21. I'm going to talk to Grant
himself about all this. 22. Of course, he will argue that
he is a good professor, but may prove only that he is a
fool. 23. He saw <u>Last Tango in Paris</u> and then tried to
explain it to the class. 24. Some of us laughed since it
seemed to us he didn't understand it. 25. But after he
finished talking one girl started crying.

38. FORMATION OF THE ASPECTS

A. <u>Perfectives Formed by Prefixation</u>. It is a commonplace
of Russian grammars to state that one means of aspectual
formation is to add a prefix to a primary (i.e., unprefix-
ed) imperfective verb to make it perfective. But at best
this is only a half-truth. It is rare that a prefix attached to a verb simply makes it perfective, without at
the same time changing its meaning to some degree. The
great majority of such perfectives have a specialized
meaning imparted by the prefix (see C below).

However, there are some common verbs in which the prefix
has no apparent meaning other than to render the verb
perfective; e.g., with по-: позвони́ть, call, ring; по-
стро́ить, build; потеря́ть, lose (not to be confused with
perfectives such as погуля́ть, поигра́ть, порабо́тать, etc.,
in which the prefix imparts the meaning of "for a while",
see 37C); with с-: сде́лать, do, make; сыгра́ть, play (note
the change of и to ы to preserve the hardness of the prefix consonant); спеть, sing.

In comparison with these two prefixes, others very rarely
lose their meaning, so that something of the special value
of the prefix remains evident, e.g. про- in прочита́ть,
read <u>through</u> (cf. пройти́, go through); раз- in рассер-
ди́ться, which implies the flaring up of anger where the
imperfective simply means "to be angry". Rather than
actually being "formed" by the addition of this or that
prefix, as if it were a regular process, such perfectives
are merely associated with their corresponding imperfectives by common usage. That is, they should be thought of
as two different lexical items closely enough related in
meaning to be considered (at least by grammarians!) an
aspectual pair. (For a fuller discussion, see Unbegaun,
<u>Russian Grammar</u>, pp. 210-228, "Formation of Aspectual
Pairs.")

B. <u>The Suffix -нуть</u> is commonly found on perfectives which
indicate a momentary or instantaneous action, suddenly
begun and ended, e.g. они́ крича́ли, imperfective, they
were shouting; but они́ кри́кнули, they cried out (and then

were silent). Other examples: двигать/двинуть, move; исчезать/исчезнуть, disappear; прыгать/прыгнуть, jump; замолкать/замолкнуть, be/fall silent; трогать/трогнуть, touch; улыбаться/улыбнуться, smile. But there are also certain verbs in which the idea of suddenness is not present, e.g. отдыхать/отдохнуть, rest, relax; привыкать/ привыкнуть, get used to.

C. <u>Imperfectives Formed from Perfectives</u>. By far the most common type of aspectual formation, and the only one which is in any way regular or predictable, is that in which the imperfective is derived from the perfective. That is, the perfective is the basic member of the pair and the imperfective is formed from it by means of a suffix or infix. The student, unfortunately, is used to thinking of the imperfective as basic because he was introduced to it first, and because most dictionaries perpetuate the misconception by giving definitions under this aspect, e.g. открывать, "open", but открыть (perf.) see открывать.

The most common and productive infix is -ыв-(-ив-). The pattern of derivation is typically as follows: For a basic verb such as писать, the "direct" perfective, which retains the same general meaning of "write", is написать. But when any other prefix is attached to this verb, it changes or specializes its meaning accordingly. Thus we have, for example, подписать, sign, and списать, copy, and the new imperfectives derived from these, which must retain the prefix, are подписывать and списывать. Other examples: играть/сыграть, play, but выиграть/выигрывать, win; проиграть/проигрывать, lose; выдумать/выдумывать, think up, invent; показать/показывать, show.

Note the change of the root vowel о to а in заработать/ зарабатывать, earn; опоздать/опаздывать, be late; осмотреть/осматривать, examine; разговорить/разговаривать, converse; устроить/устраивать, arrange (cf. строить/построить, build); and also with consonant changes in остановить(ся)/останавливать(ся), stop; спросить/спрашивать, ask.

The infix -ва-, no longer productive, is found in a certain number of verbs, e.g. дать/давать, give; встать/ вставать, get up; узнать/узнавать, find out, recognize; забыть/забывать, forget; одеть(ся)/одевать(ся), dress; открыть/открывать, open; пережить/переживать, live through, experience; убить/убивать, kill.

From many perfectives, the imperfectives are derived simply by means of a different suffix vowel, usually with a change from Conjugation II to Conjugation I: -и to stressed -а (-я after л,н,р): кончить/кончать, end; изменить(ся)/ изменять(ся) change; объяснить/объяснять, explain; повторить/повторять, repeat; получить/получать, get, receive;

продо́лжить/продолжа́ть, **continue**; реши́ть/реша́ть, **decide,
solve.** Note the consonant changes (the same as those
occurring in conjugation; see 19) in встре́тить/встреча́ть,
meet; пригласи́ть/приглаша́ть, **invite**; прости́ть/проща́ть,
forgive; употреби́ть/употребля́ть, **use**, among many others.
(The expected consonant changes do <u>not</u> occur in бро́сить/
броса́ть, **throw**; поступи́ть/поступа́ть, **enter**; **behave**;
пусти́ть/пуска́ть, **let, allow.**)

Note the exceptional pair купи́ть/покупа́ть, **buy,** in which
only the imperfective has a prefix. Often it is the perfective which has a special or irregular conjugation (see
20), while the imperfectives formed from them are quite
regular Conjugation I verbs; note назва́ть/называ́ть, **call,
name**; нача́ть/начина́ть, **begin**; помо́чь/помога́ть, **help**; по-
сла́ть/посыла́ть, **send**; собра́ть(ся)/собыра́ть(ся), **gather;
intend to**; умере́ть/умира́ть, **die**; and verbs in -нять/
-нимать, e.g. поня́ть/понима́ть, **understand.**

D. <u>Greatly Differing Forms</u>. A few aspectual pairs seem
to have very little in common, e.g. возвраща́ться/вер-
ну́ться, **return** (here even the basic root appears in different forms). There are three verbs which are reflexive
in the imperfective but not in the perfective: станови́ть-
ся/стать, **become**; **stand**; сади́ться/сесть, **sit down**; ложи́ть-
ся/лечь, **lie down.** In a few cases the imperfective and
perfective have nothing in common but their association
by usage: брать/взять, **take**; говори́ть/сказа́ть, **say, tell**;
класть/положи́ть, **put** (with other prefixes, note, e.g.
уложи́ть/укла́дывать, **pack**; but предложи́ть/предлага́ть,
offer, suggest); лови́ть/пойма́ть, **catch.**

<u>Exercises</u>. Using the information in C above as guide-
lines, form imperfectives from the following perfectives:
влюби́ться, **fall in love**; вы́держать, **stand**; **pass** (an exam);
вы́мыть, **wash out**; заказа́ть, **order**; заме́тить, **notice, re-
mark**; заме́длить, **slow**; заста́ть, **force**; изгото́вить, **manu-
facture**; изучи́ть, **learn, master**; назна́чить, **appoint**;
настоя́ть, **insist**; обрати́ться, **turn**; оправда́ть, **justify**;
отбро́сить, **throw off**; отговори́ться, **make an excuse**; от-
пра́виться, **start, set out**; отпусти́ть, **let go**; переде́лать,
alter; переписа́ть, **rewrite**; пода́ть, **serve**; подня́ть, **raise**;
приблизи́ться, **approach**; присла́ть, **send**; разви́ть, **develop**;
раздели́ть, **divide**; раздева́ться, **undress**; рассказа́ть, **nar-
rate**; сорва́ть, **tear off**; убра́ть, **remove, tidy up**; уда́рить,
hit; уничто́жить, **annihilate.**

Supply the correct forms: 1. Ва́ня никогда́ не (drank) до
войны́, а вчера́ он (drank) це́лую буты́лку вина́. 2. Ко́ля
(read) газе́ту, пока́ сестра́ (prepared) у́жин. 3. Та́ня (is
used to) храпе́нию му́жа, а я никогда́ не (will get used to)
нему́. 4. Я (was late) на уро́к, и когда́ вошёл в класс все
(started laughing). 5. Ра́йский всё (did), но ничего́ не
(got done). 6. Степа́н (has been reading) "Войну́ и мир"

ужé нéсколько мéсяцев. Он никогдá не (will finish) егó!
7. (Throw) ко мне мяч! 8. (Did you understand), когдá он
(answered) на ваш вопрóс? 9. Когдá вы (returning) в США?
--Не знáю, когдá (I will return) домóй. 10. Автóбус обык-
новéнно (stops) на э́том углу́, но сегóдня он (did not stop)
11. Кáждую суббóту лéтом мы (arranged) пикнúк. 12. Сóня
обы́чно (gets up) в семь часóв, но онá (lost) будúльник и
сегóдня (got up) в дéвять. 13. Скóлько пúсем вы (got)?
14. Онá (was buying) нóвое плáтье, когдá онá (found out),
что онó слúшком дóрого. 15. (I'll kill) тебá, (cried out)
Пáвел. Но он никогó никогдá не (killed). 16. Учёные когдá-
нибудь (will discover) нóвые истóчники питáния. 17. Не
(put) э́тих тарéлок сюдá! 18. Берёзов (lay down), а женá
(got dressed). 19. Онú (used to send) мне подáрки. 20.
"Прощáй, мой сын," прошептáл царь, "(I am dying); сейчáс
ты цáрствовать (will begin)."

Translate: 1. Alex Portnoy had just won a game of tennis
with his girl friend when he decided to take a walk around
the museum. 2. He asked the guard to show him something,
but the guard only wanted to relax. 3. He told Alex it
was forbidden to touch anything. 4. Alex examined a few
pictures, and after he had touched one of them the guard
stood up and said, "Don't touch the pictures." 5. Alex
smiled and put his hand in his pocket, but soon began
touching them again. 6. The guard got angry and repeated
his warning (предупреждéние). 7. "Sorry," answered our
hero. "I keep forgetting about that." 8. As soon as the
guard sat down by the door again, Alex quickly touched
another picture. 9. "Hey!" the guard shouted, and jumped
out of his chair. 10. At that moment Alex disappeared--
but not before he had thrown a piece of stale (чёрствый)
bread at that unhappy man as he approached. 11. It was
time to play another game with his girl friend.

39. VERBS OF MOTION

A. Indefinite-Definite Pairs. A limited number of verbs
denoting motion of one type or another have two imperfective forms, called variously "indefinite" and "definite";
"indeterminate-determinate"; "multidirectional-unidirec-
tional." Although the terms "multidirectional" (or sometimes "non-unidirectional") and "unidirectional" are the
most precise (see B below), the terms in the heading above
are used here because they are the least cumbersome. The
most important of these verbs are: ходúть/идтú, to go (on
foot); éздить/éхать, to go (in a vehicle); носúть/нестú,
to carry (by hand); возúть/везтú, convey (in a vehicle);
водúть/вестú, lead; бéгать/бежáть, run; летáть/летéть,
fly; плáвать/плыть, swim, sail. The indefinites except
for the last three and the definite летéть are of Conjugation II and have the regular consonant mutations in the
first person singular as well as (except for éздить and

летѐ́ть) the stress shift (see 19B and 21C); while the remaining indefinites are regular Conjugation I types with vowel stems and the remaining definites are more "irregular" (see 20A and C). Note that the verb е́хать has no imperative of its own; поезжа́й(те) is used.

B. <u>Basic Usage</u>. The <u>indefinite</u> member of the pair represents basically an action which is not carried out in any one particular direction. Other meanings can be seen to issue from this: the general ability indicated by the verb; motion to more than one place or in more than one direction, including to a specific place and back ("round trip"). Examples: Ива́н не мо́жет <u>ходи́ть</u>, потому́ что он слома́л себе́ но́гу, Ivan can't walk because he broke his leg; я <u>води́л</u> дру́га по го́роду, I led my friend (here and there) around the city; мы <u>е́здили</u> в теа́тр, we went to the theater (and back again).

The <u>definite</u> member represents basically an action carried out in one specific direction. This is normally although not necessarily a single action at a specific time, for if there is some reason to emphasize or individualize the action even when it is repeated or habitual, the definite rather than the indefinite can be used. Examples: сего́дня Ива́н <u>идёт</u> на рабо́ту, Ivan is going to work today; я <u>шёл</u> в теа́тр, когда́ я встре́тил дру́га, I was going to the theater when I met a friend; ка́ждый день Да́ша <u>несёт</u> кни́ги в библиоте́ку, every day Dasha carries books to the library, with pictorial emphasis on the specific action directed toward one specific goal, as compared with the more neutral and usual ка́ждый день Да́ша <u>но́сит</u>..., with logical emphasis more on repetition or habit.

Ходи́ть/идти́ are used in the general meaning of "to go" for comparatively short trips, such as those within a city, when the means of locomotion is not specified, e.g. идём к Ма́ше, let's go to Masha's. The adverb пешко́м specifies "on foot": мы хо́дим на рабо́ту пешко́м, we walk to work. When the usage of a vehicle is made explicit or implicit, as in trips to other cities or travel abroad, е́здить/е́хать must be used: мы е́здили авто́бусом, we went by bus; мы е́дем в Нью Йо́рк, we're going to New York. Note that for <u>vehicles</u> themselves, which travel under their own power, ходи́ть/идти́ are normally used: вот идёт по́езд, here comes the train. However, е́здить/е́хать are sometimes used, especially with automobiles.

C. <u>Idiomatic Usage</u>. Here the <u>definite</u> rather than the indefinite form is nearly always found. Note the usage of идти́ (and never ходи́ть) in: идёт дождь (снег), it is raining (snowing); что идёт в кино́? what's playing at the movies?; о чём идёт речь? what is the conversation about?; как бы́стро идёт вре́мя, how time flies (the literal летѐ́ть is also used here); э́та шля́па вам не идёт, that hat does not look good on you. But note the use of ходи́ть in она́ хо́дит за больны́ми, she takes care of (looks after) patients. Вести́ and not води́ть is used in он всегда́ ведёт себя́ хорошо́ (пло́хо), he always behaves well (poorly); он вёл тяжёлую жизнь, he led a hard life; везти́ and not вози́ть in the impersonal expression мне никогда́ не везёт в ка́рты, I'm never lucky at cards. Note, however, носи́ть and not нести́ in the (frequentative only) meaning of "wear" она́ обы́чно но́сит кра́сное пла́тье, she usually wears a red dress. Compare вчера́ она́ была́ (оде́та) в жёлтом пла́тье, yesterday she was (dressed) in a yellow dress.

D. <u>Perfectives and Prefixation</u>. The basic perfectives for the verbs of motion are formed by adding по- to the <u>definite</u> member. Thus: пойти́ for ходи́ть/идти́; пое́хать for е́здить/е́хать, etc. But the specific meaning of this perfective has to do with the <u>start</u> of the trip, the single direction of going there, and not the return. Compare мы пошли́ в парк, we went to (set off for) the park, and мы ходи́ли в парк, we took a walk to the park (and came back). Although the indefinite imperfective is the normal usage in this latter context, sometimes the special perfectives сходи́ть and съе́здить are found when the purpose or completion of the trip is stressed.

When any prefix other than по- is added to the imperfectives (to both forms), the meaning is specialized accordingly, with the indefinite becoming the single new imperfective and the definite the perfective. In other words, the distinction between "indefinite" and "definite" no longer exists. Thus: приходи́ть, imperfective, and прийти́, perfective, to come, arrive (приезжа́ть/прие́хать, by vehicle; note the change from е́здить); уходи́ть/уйти́ and уезжа́ть/уе́хать, go away, leave. Other important prefixed forms of "to go" are: входи́ть/войти́, come in, enter; выходи́ть/вы́йти, go out, exit; подходи́ть/подойти́, approach; отходи́ть/отойти́, move away; depart (of trains); заходи́ть/зайти́, drop in; and also, of course, the corresponding forms with -е́здить/-е́хать. N.B. that these verbs are intransitive and must be used with prepositions if the objects are mentioned, e.g. они́ прие́хали в го́род, на рабо́ту, к дру́гу, etc., they arrived in town, at work, at the friend's, etc.; мы вы́шли из зда́ния, we went out of the building; я подошёл к нему́, I approached him; по́езд отошёл от ста́нции, the train pulled away from the station. Note that all prefixed forms of идти́ become -йти́; -ойти́ after prefixes ending in a consonant; those of е́здить become -езжа́ть; also, бе́гать ＞-бега́ть; пла́вать ＞-плава́ть.

<u>Exercises</u>. Oral drills. 1. Use the appropriate form of each verb in both present and past: Я, Са́ша, сёстры сего́дня--ка́ждый день--ча́сто--по́сле обе́да (ходи́ть/идти́, е́здить/е́хать, носи́ть/нести́ кни́ги, вози́ть/везти́ дете́й, води́ть/вести́ дете́й, бе́гать/бежа́ть, лета́ть/лете́ть, пла́вать/плыть) в шко́лу.

2. Use both imperfective and perfective in present (future perfective) and past tense with all possible prepositions and objects: Я, Нина, они (пойти, поехать, приходить/прийти, приезжать/приехать, уходить/уйти, уезжать/уехать, входить/войти, выходить/выйти, подходить/подойти, отходить/отойти, заходить/зайти, находить/найти) в, на, к, из, с, от (гостиница, вокзал, брат).

Translate: 1. Where are you going? 2. I'm going to the club. 3. Do you always go to the club after school? 4. No, I sometimes go to Chicago. 5. What's going on now in Chicago? 6. There's a good play on now in the theater. 7. I went there last week. 8. I was on my way there when I ran into Tom. 9. It's always raining in California, but it almost never snows there. 10. All morning we carried things to the car, then we set out for California. 11. Do you always wear a green shirt? 12. Yes, it looks good on me. 13. Men walk, all fish swim, but some birds don't fly. 14. Yesterday I swam across the lake. 15. Last month we took a drive to the country. 16. We usually take Simon to work, but today he walked. 17. They carried on a conversation all night. 18. The boy came out of the woods and ran around the meadow for a while. 19. It's too cold, the buses aren't running today. 20. When does the train leave? 21. Alex has gone to England. 22. I don't know when he will arrive there. 23. Yesterday we dropped in on Sokolov, but when his huge dog approached us we left quickly. 24. We ran into the garage. 25. He brought his friend to me. 26. He brought eight suitcases with him. 27. He also brought a letter from Tanya. 28. Molly takes care of her mother all the time. 29. She leads a dog's life and never has any luck in anything. 30. Today she is wearing a white hat.

SUPPLEMENTARY TRANSLATION EXERCISE. Natasha is a beautiful girl. She usually wears blue or green dresses to school, but yesterday she wore a pretty little red skirt. Yesterday she was late and running to class when Steve came out of the building and caught sight of her. He went up to her and said, "Don't run so fast, your skirt is flying in the wind." Natasha blushed and walked away from him, but he ran after her and offered to carry her books. They arrived in class together. The teacher asked why they were late, and Steve told him the following story: "We were running and the wind carried away Natasha's skirt. It disappeared completely, and we finally found it high up in a tree. Of course, Natasha couldn't do anything without her skirt, so I brought it to her myself. In the meantime she had fainted (упасть в обморок). I had to dress her and then carry her into the building. That's why we're late." Poor Natasha blushed furiously and said, "Everything he told you is a lie! He never tells the truth!"

A. In the most basic usage of the reflexive verb, formed
with the suffix -ся (a contraction of себя, "oneself";
review conjugation in the Appendix), the subject receives
the action of the verb, e.g. сестра моет посуду, sister
washes the dishes, but сестра моется, sister washes (herself). A great many other verbs have both the transitive,
non-reflexive form, which takes a direct object in the
accusative, and the intransitive, reflexive form, which
cannot take a direct object. Common examples: начинать
(ся), begin; кончать(ся), end; продолжать(ся), continue;
возвращать(ся), return; одевать(ся), dress; открывать(ся),
open; with, of course, their corresponding perfectives.
Note that in English the "oneself" is generally either
superfluous or not used at all: дверь открылась, the door
opened; Иван вернулся домой, Ivan returned home.

Reminder on pronunciation: After the infinitive ending
-ть and the third person -т, the ending -ся is pronounced
with a hard с, and the preceding т is always hard, e.g.
встретиться and встретится sound alike (ending in -itsa).
After other consonant endings (шь,м,л), -ся may be pronounced either hard or soft; the -сь after vowels is soft.

B. Sometimes the reflexive indicates reciprocal action,
e.g. мы встречаемся, видимся, целуемся, прощаемся, we
meet, see each other, kiss (each other), say goodbye.
Note that when a singular subject is its own object,
себя must be used in full, e.g. он видел себя в зеркале,
he saw himself in a mirror.

C. Often the Russian reflexive has a passive meaning and
is preferred to the passive voice (see 45D), e.g. Грант
считается хорошим учителем, Grant is considered a good
teacher (the equivalent of the "impersonal" third person
plural считают Гранта хорошим учителем; also note that
with the reflexive pronoun used in its full form, Грант
считает себя хорошим учителем has the very different meaning of "Grant considers himself a good teacher"). Other
common examples: мы нашли книги на столе, we found the
books on the table, but книги находились на столе, the
books were found (situated, located) on the table; это
не так пишется, it isn't written, spelled that way.

D. Some verbs denoting mental or physical conditions are
found only in reflexive forms, in which case the suffix
has little meaning, e.g. бояться, to be afraid; гордиться,
be proud; надеяться, hope; смеяться, laugh; стараться,
try; улыбаться, smile. Other verbs denoting such conditions do have the transitive, non-reflexive forms, e.g.
беспокоить(ся), worry, bother (be worried, bothered);
занимать(ся), occupy (be occupied with, study); интересо-
вать(ся), interest (be interested in); сердить(ся), anger
(be angry). But note: я чувствую себя хорошо, I feel

well; мы чу́вствуем себя́ пло́хо, we feel poorly, etc. (чу́вствоваться means "to be felt").

E. Certain <u>impersonal</u> verbs, with the subject in the dative, are reflexive: каза́ться, to seem, and хоте́ться, to feel like, want to, among others, are used only in the third person or neuter singular: мне ка́жется, что он прав, it seems to me that he's right; ей захоте́лось петь, she had a sudden desire to sing. But the verb нра́виться, to please, appeal to, can be used in any person: э́то мне нра́вится, this pleases me; я Со́не нра́влюсь, Sonya likes me. Compare the impersonal expressions in 53C.

F. Note again that three verbs in Russian are reflexive in the imperfective but not in the perfective: станови́ть-ся/стать, stand; begin, become; сади́ться/сесть, sit down; ложи́ться/лечь, lie down. The counterparts of these verbs, indicating position or rest as opposed to motion, are not reflexive: стоя́ть, be standing; сиде́ть, be sitting; лежа́ть, be lying.

<u>Exercises</u>. Oral Drills: 1. Use both reflexive and non-reflexive forms wherever possible in combining subjects with objects: Я, Ва́ря, магази́н, собра́ние, э́то, това́рищи (беспоко́ить/ся, верну́ть/ся, встре́тить/ся, занима́ть/ся, интересова́ть/ся, конча́ть/ся, начина́ть/ся, оде́ть/ся, откры́ть/ся, серди́ть/ся) в во́семь часо́в--дверь--журна́л--кварти́ру--му́зыкой--об э́том--ребёнка--чита́ть.
2. Use the verbs in all tenses, selecting appropriate objects: Я, Со́ня, го́сти (ложи́ться/лечь, лежа́ть, сади́ться/сесть, сиде́ть, станови́ться/стать, стоя́ть) в, на (дива́н, о́чередь, посте́ль).

Translate: 1. The teacher began the lesson. 2. The lesson began at nine and ended at ten. 3. I'll return these books when I return to the city. 4. When will this store open? 5. Mother closed the window. 6. A large crowd gathered, and Grisha smiled. 7. We went into the woods to gather mushrooms. 8. Tim and Alice met each other only yesterday in the park. 9. After an hour they were kissing. 10. Later Tim was so glad that he kissed himself on the arm. 11. In the evening they quarrelled and then made up (forgave each other). 12. In the morning they dressed early. 13. They dressed each other. 14. That didn't happen, you say. 15. But that happens every day. 16. How do you say "Alice" in Russian? 17. How do you write it? 18. Where is the post office located? 19. Don't laugh, I'm worried about Sandy. 20. She's interested in drama, and that's nothing to be proud of. 21. Last night I got mad at her and felt ill. 22. She said she was going to play in "Who's Afraid of Virginia Woolf?" 23. In our family such things aren't done! 24. I hope she'll occupy herself with something else. 25. It seems to me that nowadays daughters never try to please their mothers. 26. It was getting cold, and soon it became completely

dark. 27. I got into line and waited for three hours
before I could enter the theater. 28. I wanted to sit
in the last row; I never sit closer. 29. But there were
coats lying across all the seats, and so I had to stand.
30. After an hour I felt like lying down.

41. IMPERATIVES

A. Second Person Forms: Formation. The second person
imperative is usually formed from the stem of the third
person plural. If the stem ends in a vowel, the imperative is in -й, e.g. рабо́тают/рабо́тай, work; стоя́т/сто́й,
stand, stop. For consonant stems, the ending is -и if
the ending of the first person singular is stressed, or
if the stem ends in two consonants, e.g. спеша́т/спеши́,
hurry; по́мнят/по́мни, remember. But if the stem rather
than the ending of the first person singular is stressed,
and only one consonant is involved, it is -ь, e.g. гото́-
вят/гото́вь prepare. These endings serve for the singular
and familiar form, corresponding with the usage of ты.
The plural-polite form, corresponding with вы, adds -те
to the above endings, e.g. рабо́тайте, спеши́те, гото́вьте.
Reflexive verbs add -ся after й and ь, and сь after и
and е, e.g. не бо́йся, не бо́йтесь, don't be afraid;
ложи́сь, lie down, оде́ньcя get dressed. The stress of
the imperative is the same as that of the first person
singular, e.g. пишу́/пиши́, write.

Irregular forms: Verbs with -дава́ть, -знава́ть, -става́ть
retain the infinitive stem, e.g. не встава́й don't get up.
Verbs with a present tense stem in -ь have -ей(те), e.g.
бить/бьют/бей, beat. Есть, eat, has ешь. Лечь, lie down,
has ляг, since ь is never written after a velar consonant.
For е́хать, the imperative поезжа́й is used.

B. Second Person Forms: Usage of Aspect. A very general
rule is that the perfective is used for positive commands
and the imperfective for negative commands, e.g. закро́йте
дверь, close the door; не закрыва́йте двери, don't close
the door. But there are important exceptions. If the
action indicated in a positive command is continuous
rather than specifically limited, the imperfective will
be used, e.g. the common classroom injunctions of пиши́те
and чита́йте when the teacher wants the students to be
writing or reading. The imperfective is also found in
polite commands, as in invitations: приходи́те ко мне,
come and visit me; сади́тесь, пожа́луйста, please be seated.
On the other hand, the perfective can be used in a negative command when a particular urgency or warning is meant
to be conveyed about one specific instance. Compare не
забыва́йте нас, когда́ вы бу́дете в А́нглии, don't forget
about us while you are in England, with не забу́дьте
принести́ ключи́, don't forget to bring the keys.

Note here that particularly emphatic or brusque commands may be rendered by the <u>infinitive</u>, e.g. рабо́тать! get to work!; не кури́ть, no smoking; молча́ть! be quiet! At the same time certain of these commands are more impersonal when they are directed at large audiences, as on signs, in the army, etc.

C. <u>First Person Forms</u>. These are sometimes called "inclusive" imperatives because they include the speaker. Their English equivalent is rendered with "let's..." The most common way of forming this imperative is simply to use the perfective first person plural, e.g. погуля́ем в па́рке, let's take a walk in the park; возьмём э́ти кни́ги, let's take these books. The suffix -те can be added when speaking to more than one person or in polite contexts: погуля́емте в па́рке. For verbs of motion, the definite imperfective can also be used, e.g. идём, let's go. Note the colloquial пошли́! let's be off!

For more informal or tentative suggestions, дава́й(те) and the <u>imperfective</u> infinitive are often used: дава́й(те) игра́ть, let's play. This imperfective imperative of "to give" may also be used with the first person plural perfective: дава́йте погуля́ем в па́рке. In negatives, бу́дем is used, forming an imperfective first person plural: (дава́й) не бу́дем игра́ть, let's not play. Also note: лу́чше не бу́дем игра́ть, we'd better not play.

D. <u>Third Person Forms</u>. "Let him, her, them..." is most often translated by пусть (or, more colloquially, пуска́й) with the third person of the appropriate aspect. The pronoun is sometimes omitted: пусть (он) игра́ет, let him play; пусть (она́) прочита́ет статью́, let her read the article. A further implication here is often "if he (she) wants to." The imperatives of разреши́ть and, less formally, дать, may also be used in the sense of "permit, allow" in both third and first person dative plus infinitive constructions: да́йте ему́ говори́ть, let him talk; разреши́те мне объясни́ть, allow me to explain.

<u>Exercises</u>. Oral Drill: Form imperatives for the second person (both aspects where given), using an occasional negative; for the first person, using дава́йте and/or a negative occasionally; and for the third person, using пусть (она́), and combine them with appropriate objects: Пожа́луйста, (не)/(дава́йте)(не бу́дем)/ пусть (она́) (брать/взять, не беспоко́иться, входи́ть/войти́, вымыва́ть/ вы́мыть, держа́ть, ду́мать, жить, наде́яться, отвеча́ть/отве́тить, помога́ть/помо́чь, приводи́ть/привести́, продава́ть/прода́ть, раздева́ться/разде́ться, рисова́ть, ста́вить/поста́вить, уезжа́ть/уе́хать, шить) его́--ему́--с ним--о нём

Supply the correct forms: 1. Студе́нты, (write), пожа́луйста. 2. (Write) Ната́ше сего́дня, но не (write) ей дли́нного письма́. 3. Не (be afraid of) Таре́лкина, но не (argue) с ним.

4. (Clean) э́ти о́вощи, (prepare) обе́д, и пото́м (put) э́ти таре́лки на стол. 5. (Eat), (drink) и (be merry), говори́т ста́рая погово́рка. 6. Пожа́луйста, (be seated), сказа́л хозя́ин гостя́м. (Be) как до́ма. 7. Он сказа́л своему́ сы́ну, "(lie down) спать." 8. Не (take) моего́ пера́. 9. "(Throw) мяч сюда́," кри́кнул ма́льчик, а де́вушка то́лько отве́тила, "(Kiss) меня́!" 10. Не (buy) э́того пиджака́, а (buy) тот. 11. Не (sell) ва́ши кни́ги. 12. (Finish) уро́к, пото́м (go out) на у́лицу и (play) на со́лнце. 13. (Let's go) в Нью Йо́рк. 14. (Let's not walk) здесь в па́рке. 15. (Let's write) отцу́. 16. (Let) он откро́ет окно́.

Translate: 1. "Let's drop in on the Smirnovs tonight," said Peter. 2. "Let's not go there," returned Nina. "I don't like them. 3. They have a sign in their yard which says "Keep off (don't walk on) the grass." 4. And besides, Smirnov is always saying "Don't be late to the meeting." 5. Let's call the Orlovs." 6. "Forget it, they talk too much." 7. "Let them talk; they're interesting people." 8. "Look, don't talk to me any more about them. 9. Say, are you laughing at me? All right, go ahead and laugh. 10. If you want to go there, go yourself. I'm staying home. 11. Now give me my book and let me read. 12. And don't just stand there; read something yourself!" 13. "We'd better not talk to each other any more." 14. "Then shut up and sit down."

42. CONDITIONAL EXPRESSIONS

A. Real Condition. In an actual or possible situation, one that is not contrary to fact, the simple **indicative** mood is used: он уе́хал, е́сли его́ маши́на не в гараже́, he has left if his car is not in the garage. When the conditional ("if") clause begins the sentence, то may be used to introduce the second clause: е́сли его́ маши́на не в гараже́, (то) он уе́хал. Note that in sentences like е́сли он уйдёт, (то) я то́же уйду́, if he leaves, (then) I'll leave too, the future is used in **both** clauses in Russian, where English uses the present in the "if" clause (36C).

The English "unless" is rendered in Russian by the negative е́сли...не, e.g. I can't read unless he keeps quiet, я не могу́ чита́ть, е́сли он не мо́лчит. In general, in impersonal sentences like "if we open (if one opens) the window, it will get colder in the room," е́сли is followed by the **infinitive**: е́сли откры́ть окно́, в ко́мнате ста́нет хлодне́е.

B. Unreal Condition. In a contrary-to-fact or hypothetical situation, in which the condition necessary for a certain result was not or probably could not be fulfilled in actuality, the particle бы plus the past tense of the verb is used in both clauses, e.g. она́ погуля́ла бы в па́рке, е́сли бы не́ было так хо́лодно, she would take a walk in the park if it were not so cold, or she would have taken a walk in the park if it had not been so cold (the present or past meaning here can be determined only by context).

N.B. that this conditional "would" is not the same as the "would" in tense sequences. Compare "he said he would write," он сказа́л, что он бу́дет писа́ть, and "he said he would write if he had a pen," он сказа́л, что он писа́л бы, е́сли бы у него́ бы́ло перо́.

The particle бы is always unstressed, and is sometimes shortened to б after vowels; e.g., in the "if" clause е́сли б is sometimes found. In the other clause бы normally appears after the verb or pronoun, although it may appear elsewhere if some other word is to be emphasized; compare я рабо́тал бы весь день, I would <u>work</u> all day; я бы рабо́тал весь день, <u>I</u> would work all day; я весь день бы рабо́тал, I would work <u>all day</u>.

Other clauses are possible besides those beginning with е́сли бы, e.g. на ва́шем ме́сте я бы э́того не де́лал, if I were you (lit. "in your place") I wouldn't do it; я игра́л бы с ва́ми, но не уме́ю, I'd play with you, but I don't know how.

<u>Exercises</u>. Oral Drill: match clauses appropriately, using the verbs in all possible tenses in both real and unreal conditions and supplying бы where necessary: Е́сли Та́ня (говори́т/поговори́т с подру́гой по телефо́ну, заходи́ть/зайти́ к подру́ге, ложи́ться/лечь спать, ходи́ть/идти́/пойти́ за поку́пками), то Ва́ня (корми́ть/накорми́ть ребёнка, мыть/вы́мыть посу́ду, ходи́ть/идти́/пойти́ в кино́, выходи́ть/вы́йти из до́ма)

Translate: 1. If I have time, I'll play with you. 2. If I had time, I'd play with you. 3. If I'd had time, I would have played with you. 4. But you said you'd play with us. 5. No, he said he'd play with us if he had the time. 6. You're both wrong: he said he wouldn't play with us unless he had the time. 7. What would you do if you were me? 8. If I were you I'd kiss her. 9. But if you kiss a girl she'll either laugh or get mad. 10. It would be better if you kissed her. 11. If she doesn't come I won't be able to kiss her. 12. If she hadn't come I wouldn't have been able to kiss her.

43. MODAL EXPRESSIONS WITH БЫ AND ЧТОБЫ

A. <u>Expressions of wishing, requesting, suggesting</u>. The use of бы and the past tense makes statements more tentative or polite, e.g. вы бы написа́ли ему́, you should write (or should have written) him; тебе́ сле́довало бы бо́льше занима́ться, you really ought to study more. Compare these with more direct expressions of obligation such as вам на́до написа́ть ему́, you have to write him; ты до́лжен бо́льше заниматься, you must study more. Also compare the polite я хотел бы говорить с вами, I'd like to speak with you, with the more abrupt я хочу говорить с вами, I want to talk to you. Note again the usage of бы in cases where a wish is unlikely to be fulfilled (see 42B): ты была бы здесь, I wish (would that) you were here; хорошо было бы погулять (если б не шёл дождь), it would be nice to take a walk (if it weren't raining). The verb "to be" is often omitted: хорошо бы погулять.

B. **Expressions with ни (бы...ни).** The usage of ни with interrogative pronouns or adverbs renders the indefinite meaning of "whoever, whatever", "no matter who, what", etc., e.g. что я ни делаю, мне хочется спать, whatever I do, I feel sleepy; где мы ни ходим, везде листья, no matter where we walk, there are leaves everywhere. More often, such utterances are hypothetical in tone, and and the past tense are used with the idea of "might": кто бы ни пришёл, меня не будет дома, whoever comes (might come), I won't be at home; он рад, где бы он ни жил, he's happy no matter where he lives (might live). Note also the idiom во что бы то ни стало, in any case, come what may

C. **Usage of чтобы.** Here the particle бы forms one word with the pronoun что, which is sometimes shortened to чтоб. The extended form для того, чтобы is found on occasion. It is followed by the __infinitive__ and translated "to, in order to" when the subject of the dependent clause is the same as that of the main clause, e.g. он быстро работает, чтобы кончить рано, he is working fast to (in order to) finish early. After verbs of motion, чтобы can be omitted: он пришёл говорить со мной, he came to speak to me.

Чтобы is followed by the __past tense__ and translated "so that, in order that" if the subjects of the two clauses are different, e.g. они умерли, чтобы другие могли жить, they died that (so that) others could live. This construction is used in requests after verbs like хотеть, просить, требовать, e.g. я хочу, чтобы вы пришли рано, I want you to come early. (Compare our own dialectal "I want you should come early".) N.B. that, contrary to English usage, the infinitive construction __cannot__ be used with "to want" unless there is only one subject, as in я хочу прийти рано, I want to come early.

Note some other characteristic uses of чтобы: кроме того, чтобы написать ей письмо, он и позвонил ей, besides writing her a letter he called her too; вместо того, чтобы рассердиться, он спел песню, instead of getting angry, he sang a song; нужно, чтобы мы все поцеловали невесту, It is necessary that we all kiss the bride.

Exercises. Oral Drills: 1. Transform the questions in parentheses into expressions with бы...ни: (кто говорит со мной, кого я вижу, с кем я говорю, что я делаю, чем я занимаюсь, когда я работаю, где я гуляю, куда я езжу) я всё думаю о Нине.
2. Combine the first set of verbs with appropriate uses of чтобы and the following verbs, omitting it where possible: Суворин позвонил--вошёл--хочет--требует, чтобы (вы) (обещать, ответить, помогать, сказать, читать) ему.

Translate: 1. Dear Tanya: You should have gone to New York with me. 2. I wish you were here. 3. I know I should write you more often. 4. I want you to write me, too. 5. I want to be with you soon. 6. I feel like kissing you. 7. I'd also like to hold you in my arms. 8. Dear, you <u>must</u> see New York! 9. If only it weren't raining, it would be wonderful right now. 10. And of course, it would be nice to see you too. 11. I wish summer would come! 12. No matter what you might think, I love you. 13. Wherever I am, whomever I'm with, whatever I'm doing, I always think about you. 14. I had to quit my job to come here. 15. The boss (use босс) told me not to come back. 16. I asked him to help me find another job, but he turned away (отвернуться). 17. I told him he ought to help me; in fact, I said it was his duty to help me. 18. To get a job, you know, you need a recommendation. 19. But he said I wouldn't get one from him. 20. If I'd known what a heartless man he was (бессердечный), I'd never have worked for him. 21. But I don't care; come what may, I'm going to live a happy life. 22. Instead of working somewhere, I'm going to Paris. 23. Maybe you can come yourself sometime. 24. And then it will only be necessary that we keep loving each other.

44. THE GERUND

Gerunds, perhaps more properly called "adverbial participles" in Russian, are indeclinable forms derived from verbs which describe a secondary action performed by the subject of the main verb. The traditional terminology of "present" and "past", although retained here for convenience, is somewhat misleading as explained below.

A. <u>The Present Gerund</u> is formed by adding -я (-а after the sibilants ж, ч, ш, щ) to the stem of the third person plural: читают/читая, reading; живут/живя, living; спешат/спеша, hurrying. The stress is the same as in the first person singular. Reflexive verbs add -ясь (-ась) e.g. моются/моясь, washing. Forms of -давать, -знавать, -ставать add -я to the infinitive stem, e.g. давая, giving. The gerund of быть is будучи, being. Present gerunds can be formed only from the <u>imperfective</u>; in those few cases where perfectives are used, the meaning becomes that of the past gerund (see below). The present gerund of

certain verbs, among them ждать, петь, пить, писа́ть, is
not used. It is sometimes possible to use the gerund of
a prefixed verb similar enough in meaning, e.g. ожида́я,
expecting; выпива́я, drinking (up).

The action described by a gerund is <u>relative in time</u> to
the action of the main verb. The term "present" merely
indicates that the action is <u>simultaneous</u> with that of
the main verb; thus the actual time may be present, past
or future; e.g. чита́я кни́гу, я ду́маю об Ива́не, reading
the book, I think about Ivan; чита́я кни́гу, я ду́мал об
Ива́не, reading the book, I thought about Ivan. The present gerund is the equivalent of sentences in which the
two verbs are connected with "and", e.g. и чита́ю кни́гу
и ду́маю об Ива́не, or those using conjunctions such as
когда́ я чита́ю кни́гу, я ду́маю об Ива́не, when I read a book
I think about Ivan; пока́ я чита́л кни́гу, я ду́мал об Ива́не,
while I was reading the book, I thought about Ivan.

N.B. that the Russian gerund cannot be used as a verbal
noun, as the English gerund is. Compare the above usage
of "reading" with "reading is an important activity,"
which in Russian would be rendered either by an actual
verbal noun or the infinitive used as a subject: чте́ние
(чита́ть)--ва́жная де́ятельность.

B. <u>The Past Gerund</u>, formed from <u>perfectives</u>, replaces the
past tense ending -л with -в, e.g. сказа́л, he said; and
сказа́в, having said. In literary usage the ending -вши
is still found on occasion. Reflexives must have this
more extensive ending, e.g. оде́лся, got dressed; оде́вшись,
having gotten dressed. Verbs with consonant stems which
do not have -л in the masculine singular must take -ши,
e.g. зажёг, lit; зажёгши, having lit; although these are
rare and the tendency is to avoid using them. Perfective
verbs of motion with consonant stems (those with -йти́,
-везти́, -вести́, -нести́) now form their past gerunds with
the present ending -я, e.g. вы́йдя, having gone out; при-
неся́, having brought.

The past gerund is used when the action <u>precedes</u> that of
the main verb. Compare чита́я кни́гу, я засну́л, (while)
reading the book, I fell asleep, with прочита́в кни́гу, я
засну́л, after reading (having read) the book, I fell a-
sleep. It is the equivalent of phrasing such as я про-
чита́л кни́гу и зате́м засну́л; по́сле того́, как я прочита́л
кни́гу, я засну́л.

As in English, care must be taken to avoid the "dangling
participle," in which the connection between the gerund
and the main verb is not clearly established. Note *уби́в
жену́, полисме́ны пришли́ арестова́ть Джо́нсона, having killed
his wife, the police came to arrest Johnson. This sentence has the unlikely literal meaning that the police
rather than Johnson killed his wife.

Note: a negative gerund can usually be translated as "without...", e.g. он вышел из комнаты, ничего не сказав, he left the room without saying (having said) anything.

Exercises. Oral Drills. 1. Form a gerund for each aspect and complete the sentence appropriately: (кончать/кончить работу, мыться/вымыться, одеваться/одеться, работать/поработать, сидеть/посидеть, снимать/снять номер) в гостинице, Сережа пел народную песню--вышел на улицу.

2. After having supplied the forms in the exercise below, recast the sentences wherever feasible with an appropriate conjunction, such as пока, когда, потому что, после того как.

Supply the correct forms: 1. Откровенно (speaking), я нахожу этот урок трудным. 2. (Strolling) в парке, мы увидели толпу детей. 3. (Having been late) на автобус, Сергей пошёл пешком в город. 4. Державин умер, (while working) над поэмой. 5. (Laughing), мальчик упал мёртвым. 6. (Having lived) несколько лет в Калифорнии, мы не хотим возвращаться на восток. 7. (Upon entering) в комнату, мы разделись. 8. (Having undressed), мы бросились на постель и заснули. 9. Ребёнок подошёл ко мне, почти (crying). 10. Светлов (without getting up) познакомил меня с Еленой. 11. (Being) стариком, Игорь не может бегать. 12. (Being afraid of) собак, Соня не хотела гулять там. 13. (Having met) на вокзале, они поцеловались. 14. Пётр читал нам поэму (while standing) на столе. 15. (Smoking) воспрещается. 16. Филипп изучил много новых слов (in translating: переводить) эту статью. 17. (After translating) её, он получил тридцать долларов. 18. (Working)--необходимая вещь, а (loving)--чудесная вещь.

45. PARTICIPLES

The four participles, adjectival in form and declined as such, are used far more often in the written than the spoken language. One way of distinguishing them from the adverbial participles or gerunds is that they may be replaced by phrases with the relative pronoun который, who, which, while gerunds may be rewritten only with adverbial or conjunctive phrases.

A. The Present Active Participle is formed from imperfective verbs by dropping the -т of the third person plural and adding -щий, -щая, etc., e.g. работают/работающий, working, who works; говорят/говорящий, speaking, who speaks. With reflexives, the ending is always -ся, e.g. смеющиеся, (those who are) laughing. A phrase like люди, работающие здесь is the equivalent of люди, которые работают здесь, the people who work here. But note that the participle must agree in gender, number and case with the noun it modifies, while который agrees in gender and number only, its case being determined by its usage in the clause in which it appears. In fact, when a participial phrase is rewritten this way, кото́рый is always in the nominative. Thus я говори́л с людьми́, рабо́тающими здесь, (the word order с рабо́тающими здесь людьми́ is also possible and even preferable in many contexts), but я говори́л с людьми́, кото́рые рабо́тают здесь.

Note that the participle is separated from the preceding noun by a comma, just as кото́рый is. But often participles are used as purely attributive adjectives (i.e., those standing **before** the noun), e.g., ду́мающий челове́к, a thinking man; теку́щие собы́тия, current events. Some are used all but exclusively this way, e.g. блестя́щий студе́нт, brilliant student; выдаю́щийся писа́тель, outstanding writer. Note also де́йствующий, acting, active (де́йствующее лицо́, character in a play); окружа́ющий, surrounding; подходя́щий, suitable, appropriate; сле́дующий, following, next. Finally, they may be used as nouns, e.g. уча́щийся, student (i.e., one who studies); куря́щие, smokers (i.e., those who smoke); слу́жащий, employee; заве́дующий, manager.

B. **The Present Passive Participle**, the least used of the four, can be formed only from **imperfective transitive** verbs. The adjective ending is simply added to the first person plural: лю́бим, we love; люби́мый, being loved. Theoretically, the present passive is used when the action of the participle is simultaneous with the main verb, but in practice the past passive is often used instead. Short forms in conjunction with the **passive voice** are possible, but very seldom used, e.g. кни́га (была́) чита́ема все́ми, the book is (was) being read by everyone. When a phrase such as кни́га, чита́емая все́ми, the book being read by everyone, is rewritten with кото́рый, note that the relative pronoun must be in the accusative: кни́га, кото́рую все чита́ют, the book which everyone is reading.

For the most part, original present passives are used as more or less pure adjectives, e.g. люби́мая кни́га, a favorite book. In fairly common usage are such adjectives which have English equivalents in -able or -ible; e.g. ви́димый, visible, and especially those with a fused negative particle, e.g. невыноси́мый, unbearable; незави́симый, independent; необходи́мый, necessary, indispensable (lit. unavoidable. Note also уважа́емый, respected; так-называ́емый, so-called.

C. **The Past Active Participle** is formed by adding -вший, etc. (always -ся in reflexives) after dropping the -л of the past tense: писа́ть/писа́вший and написа́вший, who was writing (has written). Verbs in -ти, -сть, -чь take -ший, e.g. нести́/нёсший, who was carrying; вести́/ве́дший, who was leading. Verbs of the идти́ family have ше́дший: найти́/наше́дший, who found. Note that verbs of either aspect may be used (the past active being the only one of the participles in which this is normally possible), depending

on whether the action is a continuous or a completed one:
он смотрел на девушку, читавшую (прочитавшую) рассказ,
he watched the girl who was reading (had read) the story.
However, the present participle читающую could be used
here in place of the past imperfective with the same force.
The equivalent with the relative pronoun is он смотрел на
девушку, которая читала (прочитала) рассказ.

A few original past actives are in frequent use as adjectives, e.g. бывший, former; прошедший, past; note also
сумасшедший, as either adjective or noun: mad(man).

D. The Past Passive Participle, the most often used of the
participles, is formed only from transitive verbs, almost
always perfective. It is used when the action of the
participle is prior to that of the main verb, e.g. эту
книгу, написанную столетие тому назад, ещё читают, this
book, written a century ago, is still being read. Short
forms are used in the predicate or in the passive voice:
книга написана, the book is, has been written; книга
была (будет) написана, the book was, had been (will be)
written. If the agent is mentioned, it must appear in the
instrumental: книга была написана Тургеневым, the book was
written by Turgenev. Rewritten with the relative pronoun,
note the accusative of который and the past perfective:
книга, которую написал Тургенев... the book, which Turgenev wrote...

The formation of the past passive, from the past tense
stem, is complicated in that there are a number of different endings. The suffix -нный is used for verbs with infinitives in -ать or -ять, e.g. прочитать/прочитанный,
read; сказать/сказанный, said; потерять/потерянный, lost;
задержать/задержанный, withheld. Note the stress shift
one syllable back in such participles.

The suffix -енный (-ённый when stressed) is used for verbs
of Conjugation II in -ить and -еть and for those so-called
"irregulars" of Conjugation I in -ти, -сть, -зть, and -чь,
e.g. положить/положенный, placed; решить/решённый decided,
solved; найти/найденный, found; унести/унесённый, carried
away. The same consonant mutations occur as in the present tense: бросить/брошенный, thrown; приготовить/приго-
товленный, prepared; сжечь/сожжённый, burned up. Note
that one -н- is dropped in the short forms, e.g. жребий
брошен, the die is cast; лучше сказано, чем сделано, easier
said than done.

The suffix -тый is used for verbs in -нуть, -оть and
-ереть, as well as monosyllabic stems (not counting prefixes) in -еть, -ить, -нть, -ять, -жать and -чать, e.g.
обмануть/обманутый, deceived; запереть/запертый, locked;
одеть/одетый, dressed; выпить/выпитый, drunk up; принять/
принятый, accepted; закрыть/закрытый, closed; начать/
начатый, begun.

Not a few past passive participles have become regular
attributive adjectives as well, e.g. вооружённый, armed;
определённый, definite (lit. defined); отвлечённый, abstract; неожиданный, unexpected; разбитый, broken; and
sometimes nouns, e.g. данные, data.

Exercises. Oral Drill: after having supplied the forms
in the exercise below, recast the sentences wherever
feasible by using который.

Supply the correct forms: 1. Человек (who is speaking) по
радио, только что был здесь в университете. 2. Вы знаете
гения, (who solved) эту задачу? 3. Задача была (solved)
гением. 4. (Solving) задачу, студент смотрел в окно. 5.
Мы видели человека (selling) карандаши. 6. (Selling)
карандаши, я встречался с разными людьми. 7. Этот мальчик
(is loved) всеми. 8. Ребята подошли к (broken) окну. 9.
Подождём (the next) поезда. 10. Вот (found) мною деньги.
11. Фёдор (is married) на Зине. 12. Вся статья уже (is
translated). 13. Балакирев теперь почти (forgotten) ком-
позитор. 14. Ты знаешь кого-нибудь (interested) музыкой?
15. Я опоздал на автобус (going) в город. 16. Я читала
газету (lying) на диване. 17. (Lying) на диване, я читала
газету. 18. (Respected) господа, начал оратор. 19. Женщина, (who was laughing) над тобой, уже вышла из комнаты.
20. Город (has been taken) неприятелем. 21. Я не знаю
(living) там девушки. 22. Гость, только что (entered) в
комнату--великий учёный. 23. Все газеты у нас (are sold).
24. Кто уже (dressed)? 25. Где (received) вами пакет?
26. Человек только тростник, но (thinking) тростник. 27.
Что вы знаете о (lost) билетах? 28. Мы кричали на людей,
(who were carrying) из комнаты стулья. 29. В нашей семье
трое (smokers). 30. Жизнь (of a drinker)--жалкое зрелище.

SUPPLEMENTARY TRANSLATION EXERCISE. Living in the United
States of America is always interesting. Living in Chicago, the so-called "Windy City," I have been in many
unforgettable places and situations. Last Friday I was
told that my favorite ballet, The Sleeping Beauty, was
playing at the opera. But to go to the opera I needed a
new coat. After having bought an expensive coat, I was
on my way to the opera when I ran into my ex-wife. Laughing at me, she said she had been deceived: never having
bought her anything or taken her anywhere, I was now buying things for myself and going to the opera. My next
wife won't be able to talk to me that way! Soon, having
sat down in my place, I was ready to see the ballet. But
then something terrible happened. I noticed that my coat,
which had just been put on another chair, was already not
there. Immediately running to the office, I told the
manager, and he and I began looking for the lost--or sto-
len--coat. In the surrounding crowd I saw a well-dressed
young man, and it occurred to me that he looked well-

dressed because he was wearing my coat! The son of a bitch, I thought. Approaching him, I asked him to return my coat, but without returning it, without even saying anything, he just walked away. He looked like a character out of a Dostoevsky novel--well-educated, perhaps, but kind of strange, wild--in a word, a madman. In trying to stop him, I touched something hard in his pocket: he was armed! While we were struggling, a policeman came up saying, "You're both under arrest!" But arriving himself, the manager told the policeman who I was. "Oh, excuse me, Mr. Senator," said the policeman, blushing. (Naturally, I had lied to the manager so he would help me find my coat.) And then my thief told us who he was: a well-known actor, whose name I don't want to tell you. But he was telling the truth, because I now recognized him. I have always considered him an outstanding actor and have seen several of his films. He had been joking, he said, and was planning to return the coat with a hundred dollars in it. To prove it, he took the hundred dollars out of the pocket, smiling broadly, and then, having given me back my coat, disappeared into the crowd. The hard thing I had felt was my own wallet and keys. The hundred dollars was mine too.

46. USAGE OF THE ADJECTIVE

A. <u>Adjectives Used as Nouns</u>. The following examples refer to <u>people</u>: ру́сский, Russian; знако́мый, friend, acquaintance; рабо́чий, worker; вое́нный, man in military service; портно́й, tailor; учёный, scientist, scholar. The last three have no feminine forms. Names which are adjectival in form, of course, change gender or number according to the person referred to, e.g. Портно́й, Mr. Portnoy; Портна́я, Mrs. Portnoy; Портны́е, the Portnoys.

Certain pronouns can function as nouns indicating people in general: ка́ждый, each; вся́кий, every; не́которые, some, a few; мно́гие, many; e.g. мно́гие из них молча́ли, many of them were silent.

The masculine noun звук is understood in гла́сный, vowel, and согла́сный, consonant (sound); the feminine noun ли́ния in пряма́я, straight line, and крива́я, curve.

The following feminine adjective-nouns refer to <u>rooms</u> (with the word ко́мната understood): пере́дняя, entrance hall; гости́ная, living room; столо́вая, dining room; ва́нная, bathroom; убо́рная, toilet. Note, however, that ку́хня, kitchen, and спа́льня, bedroom, are regular feminine nouns.

Note these <u>neuter</u> adjective-nouns: про́шлое, the past, and бу́дущее, the future (with вре́мя, time, understood); живо́тное, animal; насеко́мое, insect; жарко́е, roast meat;

сладкое, dessert; мороженое, ice cream; as well as many 79
adjectives which can be used with "thing" understood, e.g.
главное, the main thing; другое, another thing; новое, a
new thing (note also here that одно can mean "one thing").
Compare многое, much, many things, with многие, many
people.

B. Usage of Long and Short Forms. Review the formation
of the short form in the Appendix, notes on mobile vowel
in 17 and on stress patterns in 21B. Only the long form
can be used attributively, while the short form can be
used only in the predicate; compare весёлый певец, the
cheerful singer, with певец весел, the singer is cheerful,
happy. The long form may also be used in the predicate,
but there is usually a difference of meaning, however
slight. In general, the long form identifies the quality
more closely with a person or thing, implying permanence.
The word "one" could be used in the English translation.
The short form merely indicates that the quality is there
at the moment of speaking, and may be of a temporary nature. Thus, певец весёлый means "the singer is a cheerful
one (person)" while певец весел means "the singer is cheerful, happy now." In certain cases, when the quality is
considered a permanent attribute of the subject, the
translation will be different: compare Иван болен, Ivan
is ill, with Иван больной, Ivan is an invalid. In fact,
больной can be used as a noun meaning "invalid, patient".
(For a more thorough examination of the general theory of
long and short forms, see Borras and Christian, Russian
Syntax, pp. 80-88; or Ward, The Russian Language Today,
pp. 191-203.)

Only descriptive adjectives have short forms; excluded
are relative adjectives indicating time, place, nation-
ality, possession, etc., many of which have suffixes in
-ский (-ской), -овый (-овой), and the soft -ний; ordinal
numerals; active participles.

Contrary to what might be expected, it is the long rather
than the short form in contemporary Russian which is more
colloquial in tone and more often used in the predicate
when there is no appreciable semantic difference between
the two: e.g. дом новый occurs more often than дом нов
in the meaning "the house is new." The long form especially predominates in expressions having to do with color and
weather: машина красная, синяя, the car is red, blue, etc.,
сегодня погода прекрасная, холодная, today the weather is
excellent, cold, etc. But there are special cases in
which the short form is not only preferred but almost
obligatory:

C. Usage Limited to Short Form. In the following expressions, there is no real choice between the long and short
forms; the latter is used almost exclusively: ужин готов,
supper is ready; я занят (свободен) сегодня, I'm busy

(free) today; вы пра́вы, you're right; я винова́т, I'm to blame, it's my fault; бу́дьте добры́ (любе́зны), be so good, kind (as to); его́ роди́тели ещё живы́, his parents are still living; она́ хороша́ (дурна́) собо́й, she's good-looking (ugly). In most cases, the usage of the long form would entail an altogether different meaning, e.g. он свобо́дный, he is a free man; ва́ше де́ло пра́вое, your cause is just; его́ роди́тели живы́е, his parents are lively people; она́ хоро́шая (дурна́я), she is a nice (bad) person.

The usage of the short form is even more obligatory when the sentence is extended, e.g. with a prepositional phrase: я согла́сен с ва́ми, I agree with you; он гото́в к экза́мену, he is ready for the exam; она́ похо́жа на мать, she looks like her mother. However, if a verb demanding a predicate **instrumental** is used (see 27B), note the appearance of the declinable long form: e.g. она́ стано́вится похо́жей на мать, she is getting to look like her mother.

The adjective рад, glad, exists only in its short form. On the other hand, the adjectives большо́й and ма́ленкий have no short forms; those for вели́кий and ма́лный are borrowed. They may then carry the additional meaning of an **excessive** amount of the quality, as do the short forms of other adjectives indicating extent, e.g. э́та руба́шка мне велика́ (мала́), this shirt is too big (small) for me; река́ нам широка́, the river is too wide (for us to cross); ты ещё мо́лод, что́бы вести́ маши́ну, you're still too young to drive a car.

D. For the usage of **possessive** adjectives, see Section 17.

Exercises. Oral Drill: use the appropriate short forms where possible: Мне говоря́т, что Ва́ня--Ва́ря--Ва́ня и Ва́ря (больно́й, большо́й, весёлый, глу́пый, голо́дный, за́нятый, мёртвый, пья́ный, сумасше́дший, счастли́вый, учёный, хоро́ший собо́й), но я зна́ю наверняка́, что он--она́--они́ (здоро́вый, ма́ленький, угрю́мый, у́мный, сы́тый, свобо́дный, живо́й, тре́звый, ге́ний, несча́стный, рабо́чий, дурно́й собо́й).

Translate: 1. Sonya is a Russian and George is an American. 2. I'm talking about Sonya Tolstoy, the well-known scientist. 3. George says he loves her, but a few of us don't believe him. 4. She's only an acquaintance of his. 5. Yesterday they were walking around the living room and arguing with each other. 6. I think George was kind of drunk because he couldn't walk a straight line and had trouble pronouncing certain consonants. 7. I'll tell you one thing: their conversation ended only when George had to go to the bathroom. 8. The main thing is, George lives in the past, while Sonya thinks only about the future. 9. They aren't like each other at all: Sonya is pleasant while George is gloomy (угрю́мый). 10. Usually he's more dead than alive (neither alive nor dead). 11. Sonya is good-looking, but George is ugly. 12. On top of that,

his clothes are too small for him. 13. He is very big
and has an enormous appetite: yesterday he ate up an
entire roast and several desserts. 14. Now, George has
suddenly become quite merry. 15. "Why are you happy,
George?" I asked him. "Be a good guy and tell me all
about it. 16. I don't know how you can be glad. Your
father is dead, your mother is an invalid, you yourself
are so poor..." 17. "No, I'm rich," answered George.
"Rich in love. 18. Sonya is a beautiful person in many
respects." 19. "I don't agree with you. 20. And besides,
she's too young to love you." 21. "Yes, but I'm not too
old to love her!" 22. "What a foolish man you are, George!
23. Your interests are broad; hers are narrow. 24. Watch
her work; she's like an insect. 25. The world, even this
house, is too big for her. 26. If the weather is wonderful, good music is playing on the radio, and people become
happy, she notices nothing. She's stupid." 27. "You're
wrong, she's very sharp. 28. And even if she weren't so
sharp, I'd still love her because she is so sincere (и́с-
кренний). 29. "No, I think you love her because her hair
is long, her eyes big and blue, her body nice and slender."
30. "That's enough; let's talk about something else."

47. COMPARATIVES

A. **Long ("Compound") Comparatives.** When the adjective is
used in its long form before the noun, the comparative
degree is formed with бо́лее, more (or ме́нее, less): э́то
краси́вый дом, this is a beautiful house; э́то бо́лее краси́-
вый дом, this is a more beautiful house. The long form
may also be used in the predicate, as well as the short
form (see below), but here it is generally considered
bookish. If an object of comparison is mentioned, "than"
is translated by чем, e.g. э́то бо́лее краси́вый дом, чем
тот, this is a more beautiful house than that one. Note
that чем must be preceded by a comma, and that the second
term of comparison must be in the same grammatical struc-
ture as the first, e.g. у меня́ бо́лее краси́вый дом, чем
у вас, I have a more beautiful house than you (have).

B. **Short ("Simple") Comparatives.** Used more often than
the above, these are regularly formed by adding -ee to
the adjective or adverb stem. Colloquially, the ending
-ей is also found. The stress is the same as in the feminine short form (see 21B), e.g. краси́вый/краси́вее, more
beautiful; но́вый/нове́е, newer. Unlike the English simple
comparative in -er, which is formed from adjectives of
not more than two syllables and may be used anywhere,
the Russian simple comparative may be formed from a descriptive adjective of any length and is used only in the
predicate (cf. the use of the short adjective), e.g. э́тот
дом краси́вее, this house is more beautiful. When an object of comparison is mentioned, it is either in the same
case as the first and preceded by чем, or found in the

genitive: Этот дом красивее, чем тот, or этот дом красивее того. With verbs, adverbs, and prepositional phrases,
чем must be used, e.g. Светлов пишет лучше, чем говорит,
Svetlov writes better than he speaks; в столовой теплее,
чем в гостиной, it is warmer in the dining room than in
the living room. It is also used before the third person
possessive pronouns его, ее, их to avoid ambiguity: мой
дом больше, чем его, my house is bigger than his. Мой
дом больше его would mean "bigger than he is.")

C. "Irregular" Formation of Short Comparatives. Not a few
of these are formed with only one -e and the following
regular stem-consonant mutations (compare those for verbs,
19): г,д,з > ж, e.g. дорогой/дороже, dearer, more expensive; молодой/моложе, younger; к,т > ч, e.g. громкий/
громко/громче, louder; жаркий/жарче, hotter; богатый/
богаче, richer; с,х > ш, e.g. сухой/суше, drier; тихо/
тише, quieter; ск,ст > щ, e.g. простой/проще, simpler;
часто/чаще, oftener. Note the change of ё > e in лёгкий/
легче, easier, lighter. Uniquely, a "euphonic" л is added
in дешёвый/дешевле, cheaper. Certain adjectives drop -к
or -ок, and then undergo the regular consonant changes,
e.g. близкий/ближе, closer; высокий/выше, higher; корот-
кий/короче, shorter; низкий/ниже, lower; редкий/реже,
more seldom; also note широкий/шире, wider.

Among the truly irregular comparatives, with unpredictable
changes, are глубокий/глубже, deeper; сладкий/слаще, sweet-
er; далеко/дальше, further; долго/дольше, longer (in time);
тонкий/тоньше, thinner, finer; рано/раньше, earlier; позд-
но/позже, later. Старый, old, has two comparatives with
different meanings: the regular старее for things in general, and старше for comparing the relative ages of
people. As in other languages, some of the most commonly
used comparatives are based on entirely different roots:
хороший, good, and лучше, better; плохой, bad, and хуже,
worse. The comparative for both большой and великий is
больше, bigger, greater, which also serves as the comparative for много, much, many; for маленький and малый it is
меньше, smaller, lesser, which also serves as the comparative for мало, little, few.

D. Special Comparatives. Before nouns and verbs, больше
and меньше rather than более and менее are used: у него
больше книг, чем у вас, he has more books than you (note
that больше, as other quantitative adverbs, must be followed by the genitive of the noun; see 24B); вы читаете
меньше, чем я, you read less than I do.

An emphatic comparative may be rendered with гораздо, much,
by far: Соня гораздо умнее Саши, Sonya is much smarter than
Sasha. The question "by how much, how much more" is на
сколько, and the answer is given with на and the accusative, e.g. на сколько он старше тебя, How much older is
he than you? Он старше меня на три года, he is three years

older than me. The prefix по-, when added to the short
comparative, gives the meaning "somewhat more": нарéжьте
мя́со потóньше, slice the meat somewhat thinner. The idea
of "as much as possible" is rendered by как мóжно or воз-
мóжно with the comparative: придúте ко мне как мóжно
скорée, come to me as soon as possible. "More and more"
is всё бóльше и бóльше; likewise, with other comparatives,
e.g. всё грóмче и грóмче, louder and louder. "Even more,
still more" is ещё: он стал говорúть ещё грóмче, he began
to talk even louder, louder yet.

"As...as" is translated by так (же)...как (и): онá так
(же) умнá, как (и) он, she is as smart as he is. The emphatic particles же and и are not used in negative constructions: онá не так умнá, как он. "The...the" is
чем...тем: чем бóльше я читáю, тем мéньше пишý, the more
I read, the less I write. Note the translation of тем
when used alone: тем лýчше, all the better (or so much
the better).

<u>Exercises.</u> Oral Drills: use the correct short compara-
tive forms: 1. Моя́ квартúра (блúзко, большáя, далекó,
дорогáя, интерéсная, мáленькая, нóвая, плохáя, прекрáсная,
стáрая, хорóшая), чем вáша.
2. Сейчáс на дворé жáрко--прохлáдно--свежó--светлó--темнó--
тúхо--хóлодно, но (рáно, пóздно) бы́ло/бýдет ещё (---).

Translate: 1. In his garden Victor has more beautiful
flowers than I do. 2. It's true that I have fewer beautiful flowers. 3. But his flowers aren't more beautiful
than mine. 4. I have a more beautiful flower than he
does. 5. I'm talking about a flower more beautiful than
the flowers you know. 6. She is softer than the rose,
fresher than the green grass, and she sings more sweetly
than the birds. 7. Varya is older than me but five years
younger than Tanya. 8. She has an old grandmother, far
older than mine. 9. This grandmother is always saying,
"Speak louder," since she is becoming deafer and deafer.
10. I see Varya more often than I see my own mother.
11. The more I say it, the more I hate myself, but Varya
is closer to my heart. 12. It's better not to talk about
it. 13. She is a simpler girl than Tanya, but so much
the worse for Tanya. 14. Her grandmother says she is as
quiet as a cloud. 15. She can even drive a car this
quietly. 16. According to the old Russian proverb (по-
слóвица): "The quieter you ride, the further you'll be."
17. Here Tanya is worse; she always drives as fast as
she can. 18. I don't care what they say, I'm richer than
Victor. 19. He may have millions, but he is not as rich
as people think. 20. His interests are lower and narrow-
er (ýзкий) than mine. 21. In other words, mine are higher and broader. 22. He has his flowers, but I have something much dearer. 23. But here is perhaps a more
interesting question. 24. If Victor is so rich, why does
he always say when he is buying things, "Show me something
cheaper"?

A. <u>Compound Form</u>. This is the most common way of forming
the superlative. The adjective сáмый appears before the
long form of the adjective and agrees with it in gender,
number and case: мы живём в сáмом красúвом дóме в гóроде,
we live in the most beautiful house in town. Note the
use of из plus the genitive plural to translate "of":
сáмый красúвый из домóв, the most beautiful of the houses.

B. <u>Simple Form</u>. The suffix -ейший (-áйший after the velars
г,к,х with regular mutations to ж,ч,ш) is added to the adjective stem, e.g. нóвый/новéйший, newest; велúкий/вели-
чáйший, greatest. As adjectives, they are of course fully
declinable. When an actual comparison is made or implied,
the compound form is now almost always used in preference
to the simple. But a high degree of some quality with no
particular object of comparison is rendered by the simple
form; compare вот сáмая красúвая птúца, here is <u>the</u> most
beautiful bird, and вот красúвейшая птúца, here is a most
beautiful bird. The simple form often has emotional color-
ing. It is also found in certain idioms, e.g. важнéйшая
роль, major (i.e., a most important) role; с величáйшем
удовóльствием, with the greatest pleasure; нет ни малéй-
шего сомнéния, there's not the slightest doubt. The force
of the superlative has been lost altogether in дальнéйший,
further, subsequent.

C. <u>Special Superlative Pairs of Adjectives</u>. Лýчший can
mean "better" or "best"; хýдший "worse" or "worst", depending on context, e.g. он лýчший студéнт, чем онá, he is
a better student than she is; but он мой лýчший студéнт,
he is my best student. Вúсший and нúзший usually have the
superlative meanings of "highest" and "lowest", e.g.
нúзшая температýра мéсяца, the lowest temperature of the
month. But note: вúсшее образовáние, higher education;
вúсшее (not высóкое) óбщество, high society. (Perhaps
logically enough, "high school" is in Russian срéдняя
шкóла, i.e., "middle school"). Млáдший and стáрший mean
"youngest", "eldest", or "younger, elder" if only two
people are compared: Сáша--млáдший из моúх детéй, Sasha is
the youngest of my children, but мой млáдший брат, my
younger brother. They can also mean "junior" and "senior".

The superlative meaning of the above can be emphasized by
adding сáмый: он сáмый лýчший студéнт в клáссе, he is the
very best student in the class. In this context, the bookish prefix наи- is sometimes found, e.g. с наилýчшими
пожелáниями, with very best wishes.

Exceptions to the above are бóльший and мéньший, which can
be used only as comparatives meaning "greater" and "lesser".
Note that in the instrumental singular (masculine-neuter)
and in the plural only the stress differentiates бóльший
and большóй.

D. **Superlatives with** всего **and** всех. The **adverbial** superlative is expressed by the simple comparative plus всего,
referring to actions and things, or всех, referring to
people: он лучше <u>всего</u> играет в шахматы, he plays chess
better than anything else (i.e., any other game); он
лучше <u>всех</u> играет в шахматы, he plays chess better than
anyone (i.e., all other people).

Exercises. Oral Drill: use the adjectives in the positive,
comparative, and superlative degrees in singular and plural:
Мы осмотрели—сделали снимки—ходили по—познакомились с—
бывали в (более / самый) (дорогой, известный, интересный,
прекрасный) (гостиница, ресторан) чем вы / в городе

Translate: 1. Dearest Misha: The most interesting thing
has happened to me. 2. I've met a boy who considers himself the smartest student in school. 3. He said he was
not only the smartest student in high school too, but also
the fastest reader. 4. I don't know whether he is the
best student, but he certainly has the biggest ego (я).
5. You meet this kind of character in higher education,
but most often in high society. 6. His name is Harold
Frank, Jr. 7. His father is one of the most famous scien-
tists in Germany. 8. He played a major role in the dis-
covery of—I don't remember exactly what, but it's something <u>very</u> new. 9. Maybe he's the greatest scientist
living now. 10. Harold told me I was the most beautiful
of the girls here. 11. I accepted his invitation to a
party with the greatest pleasure. 12. My older sister
warned me not to go anywhere with him, and I soon found
out how right she was. 13. Without the slightest doubt,
it was absolutely the worst experience of my life. 14.
When he tried to kiss me I ran away from him, but he could
run faster than I could—faster than anyone, it seemed—
and he caught me in the woods. 15. Further developments
with this beast I don't want to tell you about, Misha
sweetest. 16. Speaking about <u>our</u> relationship (отношения,
pl.), this is of course more important to me than anything. 17. We are the closest of friends, and you will
always be closer to my heart than anyone. 18. With the
sincerest love and very best wishes, Tanya.

49. NUMERALS

A. **Cardinal Numerals.** Review the declensions in the Appendix. Case requirements after cardinal numerals are as
follows. When the numerals are in the nominative or
accusative case:

After <u>one</u> (which has all three genders in singular and a
plural, like adjectives and pronouns) and all of its compounds except 11, the noun and any modifiers are in the
nominative or accusative singular, e.g. сорок одна хорошая комната, 41 good rooms; мы осмотрели сорок одну

хорóшую кóмнату, we looked at 41 good rooms. Note that "one" is generally not expressed in phrases like рабóтать час, to work for one hour. In counting, "one, two, three," etc., is <u>раз</u>, два, три, etc.

After 2, 3, 4 and their compounds, except 12, 13, 14, the noun is in the <u>genitive singular</u> while the adjective is in the <u>genitive plural</u>, e.g. двáдцать три хорóших кóмнаты, 23 good rooms. With feminine nouns after these numerals, the adjective may also be in the nominative plural (23 хорóшие кóмнаты. Note the use of the nominative plural when a pronoun or adjective appears <u>before</u> any numeral greater than one: я прочитáл вáши три ромáна, I have read your three novels; я рабóтал пéрвые пять часóв, I worked the first five hours. It should also be noted that 2, 3, and 4 normally have the animate accusative-genitive, but not in compounds, e.g. он знáет черырёх механика, he knows four mechanics; but он знáет двáдцать четúре механика, he knows 24 mechanics.

The same requirements apply for óба, both, and полторá, one and a half. Note that "both of us, both of you," etc., is rendered мы óба, вы óба; i.e., "we both, you both." Both два and óба have special forms used with feminine nouns: две, óбе. The entire declension of the latter is so differentiated (see Appendix).

After 5 through 20, 25 through 30, 35 through 40 and up, <u>both</u> noun and adjective are in the <u>genitive plural</u>, e.g. семнáдцать хорóших кóмнат, 17 good rooms.

When the numeral stands in an <u>oblique</u> case (any case other than the nominative-accusative), the noun and its modifiers must be in the same case, always in the plural except after "one": мы ходúли по однóй хорóшей кóмнате, we walked around one good room; по шестú хорóшим кóмнатам, around six good rooms.

<u>Approximation</u> can be expressed either by óколо with the genitive, or, more colloquially, by placing the numeral after the noun: óколо шестú кóмнат, or кóмнат шесть, about six rooms.

B. <u>Collective Numerals</u>. Only двóе, трóе, and чéтверо are in common use in modern Russian. Unlike два, три, четúре, they require the genitive <u>plural</u>, unless they stand in an oblique case, when the rules would be the same as for the cardinal numerals (see the declensions in the Appendix). Their usage is obligatory with nouns having only a plural form (see 11A), e.g. чéтверо нóжниц, four pair of scissors. Their usage is preferred but not obligatory with adjectives used as nouns, e.g. трóе больнúх, three patients. They are found idiomatically or colloquially in such contexts as нас бúло трóе, there were three of us; трóе детéй (rather than the usual три ребёнка, three children.

Adverbs denoting comparisons of quantity are formed by prefixing в- to the collectives: вдвбе, twice as; втрбе, three times as, etc: он читáет вдвбе бóльше, чем я, he reads twice as much as me. Beginning with "five," the forms в пять раз, в шесть раз etc., are used.

Note that the adverbs of quantity мнóго, мáло, немнóго, скóлько and нéсколько are declined in the oblique cases (see Appendix), e.g. я пошёл в кинó с нéсколькими друзьями, I went to the movies with several friends.

C. <u>Agreement of Subject and Verb</u>. The usage of the singular (neuter past) is normal with numerals followed by inanimate nouns, and with the adverbs мнóго, мáло, etc: двáдцать (мнóго) книг лежúт (лежáло) на столé, twenty (many) books are (were) lying on the table. With nouns referring to people, however, the plural is normally used: шесть человéк идýт (шли) по ýлице, six men are (were) going along the street.

D. <u>Ordinal Numerals</u>. For a list of ordinals, one to one million, with their proper stresses, see Appendix. Note well that these are used as <u>adjectives</u>, and as such are <u>not</u> followed by the genitive: пятый урóк, not *пятый урóков, the fifth lesson. Review the special declension of трéтий, third (like that of чей, whose). In compound ordinals, only the final element has the ordinal form, e.g. сóрок шестóй урóк, 46th lesson. Во-пéрвых (вторы́х) mean "in the first (sedond) place."

<u>Fractions</u> are expressed by cardinals with ordinals, e.g. однá пя́тая, one-fifth; три восьмы́х, three-eights (the feminine noun часть, part, is understood). But: половúна, half; треть, third; чéтверть, fourth, quarter. "Half an hour" is полчасá.

<u>Exercises</u>. Oral Drills. 1. Decline the numerals and objects as necessary: Светлóв(у) нýжен (нужнá, нужны́)-- пригласúл--написáл--говорúл с--игрáл при--(1, 2, óба, 3, 5, 8, 12) (знаменúтый актёр, красúвая жéнщина).
2. Use <u>ordinal</u> numerals: Сейчáс мы читáем (1,2,3,4,5,6, 7,8,9,10,11,12,15,20,23,30,34,40,45,50)(урóк, главá)

Translate: 1. One hat. 2. One table. 3. 11 tables. 4. 21 tables. 5. 61 tables 6. 61 long tables. 7. 32 red cars. 8. 12 blue cars. 9. Both green cars. 10. Both of them have disappeared. 11. I held the book with both hands. 12. Three living rooms. 13. Six living rooms. 14. They worked for one week. 15. 47 great men. 16. 19 years. 17. 20 years. 18. 31 years. 19. 34 years. 20. We saw one black bird. 21. We saw two black birds. 22. We saw one tall man (three tall men, five tall men, 22 tall men). 23. We saw many people there. 24. Many people were there. 25. He talked about seven different girls. 26. He talked about many girls. 27. They had seen all three cars.

28. He went to all three brothers. 29. He went to the third brother. 30. In this hotel there are about a hundred rooms. 31. Two gates. 32. Eight gates. 33. Three clocks. 34. 31 clocks. 35. There were four of us on the field. 36. He ran twice as fast as me. 37. This road is ten times as long as that one. 38. The fourth month. 39. The ninth month. 40. In the third place. 41. The 50th year. 42. The 51st year. 43. On the 17th floor. 44. Two-thirds. 45. Three-fourths. 46. Five-sixths.

50. TIME EXPRESSIONS I

A. Time of Day. "What time is it?" is in general который час?, or, more colloquially, сколько (сейчас) времени? "At what time?" is correspondingly в котором часу?, or во сколько?

"One o'clock" is simply час, not один час. Note the following: 2:00 A.M., два часа ночи, 5:00 A.M, пять часов утра, 12:00 P.M. (noon), двенадцать часов дня or полдень; 4:00 P.M., четыре часа дня; 6:00 P.M., шесть часов вечера; 12:00 A.M. (midnight), двенадцать часов ночи or полночь. N.B. that Russian consistently uses вечер for the social or waking part of the evening (until 12:00 or so), while we often use "night."

When minutes are indicated Russian refers to the coming hour: 3:01, одна минута четвёртого (literally, "one minute of the fourth hour"); 3:05, пять минут четвёртого; 3:15, четверть четвёртого ("a quarter of the fourth"); 3:30, половина (colloquially often shortened to пол) четвёртого; 3:45, без четверти четыре ("without a quarter four"); 3:55, без пяти четыре. N.B. the use of the ordinal before the half-hour; the cardinal afterward. In the past tense, было is used except with час alone or одна минута, where the verb must agree; было три часа, it was three o'clock; but был час, it was one o'clock. In the future, будет is always used.

In the "official style," as in transportation schedules, the time is given just as we give it: 9:03, девять три; 9:15, девять пятнадцать; 9:45, девять сорок пять, etc., except that the hours P.M. are from 13 to 24, e.g. 3:15 P.M. = 15:15.

"At" is translated by в plus the accusative: в час, at 1:00; в два часа, at 2:00; в четверть третьего, at 2:15, etc. An exception: половина appears in the prepositional: в половине третьего, at 2:30. However, simply половина (пол) третьего may also be used here. Before без, в is usually omitted: без четверти три, at 2:45.

Note the following expressions: ровно в два часа, at 2:00 sharp; часы спешат (отстают) на пять минут, the clock is five minutes fast (slow).

B. **Day, Month and Year.** "What is today's date" is котóрое (or more often, какóе) сегóдня числó? And for the answer, e.g. сегóдня тринáдцатое сентябрá, today is the 13th of September. (The neuter noun числó is understood but not expressed after the ordinal.) "On" is expressed simply by the genitive without a preposition: какóго числá? On what date? тринáдцатого сентябрá on Sept. 13.

"In" a certain year is translated by в and the prepositional, with only the final ordinal element and the word "year" declined: "in 1956" would be written in Russian в 1956-ом годý and read aloud в тысяча девятсóт пятьдесят шестóм годý. Note that the case ending on the ordinal is written out and "year" expressed (often shortened to г. in writing); also that Russian does not use the "teens" here as we do: "one thousand nine hundred" rather than "nineteen hundred." "On Sept. 13, 1956" is 13-го сентябрá 1956-го гóда (тринáдцатого сентябрá тысяча девятсóт пятьдесят шестóго гóда). Note that everything here-- date, month, ordinal and the word "year"--is in genitive.

Decades are expressed with ordinals and the plural of "year", and "in" with в and the prepositional, e.g. двадцáтые гóды, the twenties; в двадцáтых годáх, in the twenties.

In expressions of **age**, Russian uses **dative** construction: скóлько вам лет? How old are you? (Lit. "how many years to you?"). Мне сóрок два гóда, I am forty-two. Note the expression of "and a half" here and in other contexts: мне семь с половúной, I am seven and a half.

Exercises. Oral Drills: give all possible answers to the following questions: 1. Котóрый час? 2. Какóе сегóдня числó? 3. Когдá это случúлось? 4. Скóлько тебé лет? (1:00 A.M., 3:00 A.M., 6:00 A.M., 11:00 A.M., noon, 2:00 P.M., 7:00 P.M., midnight, 3:01, 3:05, 3:10, 5:15, 5:30, 5:45, 6:50, 6:57; Jan. 1, Apr. 3, May 10, Sept. 4, Nov. 19, Dec. 28; 1861, 1965, 1970, 1972; Oct. 12, 1492, Dec. 7, 1941, Nov. 22, 1963; 4, 7, 9½, 13, 21, 38, 54, 80, 110)

Translate: 1. It is midnight. 2. 1:15 A.M. 3. 6:30 A.M. 4. 6:03 P.M. 5. 2:29 P.M. 6. 2:31 P.M. 7. It was 11:40. 8. It was 7:01. 9. It will be 10:00. 10. A quarter to one at night. 11. What time did you come? 12. I came at one. 13. At 7:30 in the evening. 14. At 7:45 sharp. 15. At noon. 16. I worked 15 minutes. 17. I worked eight and a half hours. 18. My watch is 45 minutes fast, and yours is about ten minutes slow. 19. It is now 4:57, said the voice on the radio. 20. What is the date? 21. It's June 24. 22. April 19. 23. December 3, 1973. 24. In what year were you born? 25. I was born in 1949. 26. George Washington was born February 22, 1732 and died December 14, 1799. 27. Both John Adams and Thomas Jefferson died on July 4, 1826. 28. How old were they? 29. Washington

was 67, Adams was 91, Jefferson was 83.   30. Although
Mozart died in his thirty-sixth year, he wrote more than
600 pieces, and today his music is just as popular as it
was in the 19th century, or in the thirties, forties,
fifties and sixties of this century.

51. TIME EXPRESSIONS II

A. "On" is translated by в and the accusative with days
of the week: e.g. в понедельник, во вторник, в среду,
on Monday, Tuesday, Wednesday. N.B. that days of the week
as well as months are not capitalized in Russian. Holi-
days take на and the accusative: на Рождество, на Пасху,
on Christmas, Easter. Note the use of на and the prepositional in на этой неделе, this week; на прошлой неделе,
last week; на будущей неделе, next week). Note also the
expressions на следующий день (accusative), the next day;
на днях (prepositional plural), the other day.

Habitual action is expressed by по and the dative plural,
e.g. по воскресеньям мы ходим в парк, On Sundays we go to
the park.

In general, "in" with larger units of time is translated
by в and the prepositional: в апреле (месяце), in (the
month of) April; в будущем году, next year; в 18-ом веке,
in the 18th century. Also note в детстве, старости, in
childhood, old age; в начале, конце, at the beginning,
end. But the accusative is used in в это время, at this
time; в этот момент, at this moment; в последнее время,
recently. "Ago" is тому назад, e.g. три месяца тому
назад, three months ago.

B. The instrumental without a preposition is used with
periods of the day and seasons: утром, днём, вечером,
ночью, in the morning, during the day, in the evening, at
night; весной, летом, осенью, зимой, in the spring, summer, fall, winter. "In the afternoon" can be rendered by
днём or после обеда. Note the translation of "this" in
"this morning, evening": сегодня утром, вечером (вчера
утром, yesterday morning; завтра вечером, tomorrow evening).

"Every..." is always каждый and the following time in the
accusative, without a preposition, e.g. каждое лето мы
ездим в деревню, every summer we go to the country; они
встречались каждую неделю, they met every week.

C. "For" followed by a certain period of time when the
action expressed by the verb is simultaneous with the
period is translated by the accusative without a preposition, e.g. он работал неделю, he worked (for) a week.
When "for" cannot be omitted in English--i.e., when the
action of the verb precedes the period of time--на is used
in Russian, e.g. мы поехали в деревню на неделю, we drove

to the country for a week; я взял вáшу машúну на два
часá, I took your car for two hours. The corresponding
question is на скóлько врéмени? for how long? Notice
in combination with adverbs: надóлго, for a long time;
навсегдá, forever.

"In, during" is translated in various ways. В or за plus
the accusative stresses the period of time necessary to
complete an action: я написáл э́тот расскáз в (за) три
недéли, I wrote this story in three weeks. Чéрез means
"after (a certain period has elapsed)": онá уéхала чéрез
недéлю, she left in (after) a week. "By" a certain time
is translated with к, e.g. он приéдет к пя́тнице, he will
arrive by Friday. Во врéмя translates "during" when used
with activities or historical events: во врéмя еды́, during a meal; во врéмя войны́, during the war. (Note that
вó-врéмя, sometimes written as one word, means "on time":
мы пришлú на собрáние вó-врéмя, we arrived at the meeting
on time.) В течéние with the genitive means "during, in
the course of": в течéние гóда, in the course of a year.
В and the accusative renders "per, (in) a": три рáза в
недéлю, three times a week.

"Since" is translated by с: я живу́ здесь с апрéля, I have
been living here since April. "From...to" is с...до:
с утрá до вéчера, from morning to evening; or от...до
when more specific times or dates are mentioned, e.g. от
двух до пятú часóв, from 2:00 to 5:00. С...по gives the
inclusive meaning "from...through"; с сентября́ по декáбрь
from September through December. Note the accusative with
по here. "From time to time" is врéмя от врéмени.

Exercises. Oral Drill: answer the question with the possibilities below: Когдá вы рабóтали там? Use the future
(я бýду or мы бýдем рабóтать там...) occasionally and/or
where necessary: (4 hours, 8 hours, from 8:00 to 5:00,
from 10:00 to 3:00; in the morning, in the afternoon, at
night, yesterday evening, this morning; all day, all morning, every day, every night; mornings, evenings, nights;
Monday, Tuesday, Wednesday; Thursdays, Fridays, Saturdays;
from Monday to Saturday, from Wednesday through Saturday;
once a week, twice a week, 3 times a month, 5 times a
month; this week, last week, next week, last month, next
month; from March to October, from May through August,
from June 1 to September 21; in the spring, summer, fall,
winter; last year, next year; 2 years ago, 5 years ago)

Translate: 1. During the day, I usually see Dolly on
Tuesdays and Thursdays. 2. But this week she wasn't in
class on Tuesday. 3. Friday evening we went to the opera.
4. Over the weekend we studied French together. 5. We
have an exam next week, on Thursday morning. 6. At the
present time I know very little French. 7. But Dolly said
at the beginning of the course in September that I knew
how to French kiss very well. 8. In one week, seeing her

every night, I became very well acquainted with her. 9.
This morning I studied my lesson for four hours, but during class I could think only about Dolly. 10. Later I
went downtown for a couple of hours and thought about what
we would do in the evening. 11. In the fall it was perhaps five times a month, and now in March it's about five
times a week. 12. She was thinking about the same thing
yesterday evening: "Let's do something else tomorrow evening," she said. 13. From time to time I saw myself in
store windows and broke out laughing, because I looked
like somebody who lived in the last century. 14. Last
summer Dolly was in Paris while I was in New York. 15.
She says it is wonderful in Paris from spring to fall.
16. They say it's okay there even in the winter. 17. If
only I had been there with her last year: what we could
have done! 18. We'll probably go there together in two or
three years. 19. For how long, you ask? 20. Say, from
June to September, or perhaps forever. 21. I must see
Paris in the springtime! 22. And I would like to see it
every springtime! 23. But at the moment another need calls
me, and I won't be able to meet Dolly on time. 24. I was
supposed to be at her place by 8:00. 25. The other day
she was mad at me for being late. 26. And when Dolly is
mad at me I might as well (с тем же успéхом) wait for
Christmas.

52. IMPERSONAL EXPRESSIONS I

A. The Adverb. By itself, without a subject, the adverb
may be a complete sentence in Russian, e.g. хорошó, it is
good; теплó, it is warm; трýдно, it is difficult. The
English "it" in such a context is not translated. Comparatives may also be used in this way: e.g. теплéе, чем
вчерá, it is warmer than yesterday. For the past and
future, бы́ло and бýдет are used: трýдно бы́ло (бýдет), it
was (will be) difficult. When such expressions are made
personal, the pronoun is put into the dative: мне хорошó,
things are well for me; емý трýдно, it is difficult for
him; нам скýчно бы́ло, we were bored, etc. N.B. that
English constructions with nominative subjects will, if
translated into Russian this way as beginning students
often do, give meanings different from those intended,
e.g. я холóдный, "I am a cold person" rather than "I feel
cold"; мы скýчные, "We are boring people" rather than "we
are bored."

Quantity words such as мнóго, мáло, нéсколько, etc., are
used in subjectless sentences, without the English "there
is (are)" being translated, e.g. здесь мнóго людéй, here
there are many people; мáло бýдет воды́, there will be
little water. A few noun forms are used this way: note
порá, it is time (to); жаль plus the accusative in the
meaning of "to be sorry for": нам порá идти́, it's time
for us to go; мне жаль вáшего брáта, I feel sorry for
your brother.

B. **Expressions of Possibility and Necessity.** Мо́жно has
the double meaning of "it is possible (to)" and "one may,
is permitted (to)": мо́жно игра́ть в футбо́л под дождём, it
is possible to play soccer in the rain; ей мо́жно бы́ло
игра́ть на роя́ле, she was permitted to play the piano.
Возмо́жно is synonymous with мо́жно only in the meaning "it
is possible." The opposite is нельзя́, it is impossible
(to), one may not, is forbidden (to), with невозмо́жно a
synonym only in the first meaning. Do <u>not</u> use *не мо́жно
instead of нельзя́. When made personal, with the pronoun
in the dative, мо́жно and нельзя́ normally carry only the
meaning of permission granted or denied, as in the second
example above. In the meaning of possibility or ability
they are replaced by the verb мочь (не мочь), e.g. мы
мо́жем игра́ть в футбо́л под дождём, we are able to play
soccer in the rain.

With verbs, <u>need</u> is expressed by на́до (or slightly more
formally, ну́жно): на́до (ну́жно) откры́ть окно́, it is necessary to (one must) open the window; мне на́до (ну́жно) бы́ло
рабо́тать весь день, I had to work all day. To emphasize
<u>moral obligation</u>, the short adjective до́лжен (должна́,
должны́) is used, with the subject in the nominative, e.g.
ты до́лжен писа́ть ма́тери, you must, ought to write your
mother; мы должны́ бы́ли убира́ть ко́мнату, we had to clean
up the room. These are not, properly speaking, impersonal
expressions, since subject, verb and predicate are expressed and in agreement. До́лжен may also mean "is due," as
in по́езд до́лжен прийти́ в семь часо́в the train is due to
arrive at seven o'clock; ско́лько я вам до́лжен? how much
do I owe you? The conjectural "must" is expressed by
должно́ быть, e.g. он, должно́ быть, ушёл, he must have left.

With <u>nouns,</u> need is expressed by the short adjective
ну́жен, нужна́, ну́жно, нужны́, agreeing with the thing that
is needed, with the person in the dative, e.g. мне нужна́
кни́га, I need a book (lit., "to me a book is needed");
им нужны́ бы́ли карандаши́, they needed pencils. In other
words, the subject of the Russian sentence is the thing
needed. Colloquially, the unchangeable form на́до (ну́жно)
is often used, with a verb such as име́ть, "to have," understood and the thing needed accordingly in the accusative, e.g., мне на́до (име́ть) кни́гу, I need (to have) book.

<u>Exercises.</u> Oral Drill: Make appropriate combinations of
I, II, and III in past and future as well as present, declining or conjugating wherever necessary: I. Я, ты, он,
она́, мы, вы, они́ II. ску́чно, хо́лодно, пора́, мо́жно, нельзя́,
(не) мочь, на́до, до́лжен, ну́жен (быть) III. на собра́нии,
идти́ на собра́ние, игра́ть на у́лице, писа́ть ма́тери, чи́стить
о́вощи, чемода́н, шля́па, пальто́, де́ньги

Translate: 1. It was too hot in the room. 2. It was also
very boring, since Smirnov was there. 3. It was hard for
me to breathe with everyone smoking. 4. "You're okay,"

said Smirnov, blowing smoke in my face, "you're a non-smoker." 5. "Well, it's time to go home," I muttered. (пробормотать) 6. "Why do you have to go home so soon?" Smirnov wanted to know. 7. "My wife is waiting for me," I replied. "She misses (is bored without) me." 8. "She must love you," Smirnov said with a laugh. 9. I suddenly felt sorry for him. 10. No one likes him; it's impossible to like him. 11. But everyone needs friends. 12. A good friend should tell you when, how and why you are wrong. 13. "If you need a friend," I said to Smirnov, "try and find one." 14. Being drunk, Smirnov threw his vodka at me, but there were several people around me and it hit the hostess right in the face. 15. Smirnov was asked to leave, and after that he could not come back there again. 16. What a pity, I thought with a smile. 17. I can go to Suzanna's whenever I want. 18. One might say everyone likes me. 19. But in order for people to like Smirnov, he will need a new personality (личность). 20. He could also use a new face.

53. IMPERSONAL EXPRESSIONS II

A. Omission of Pronoun. In this way, the second person singular or the third person plural can be used impersonally (see 31A). With the former, the effect is often proverbial, e.g. тише е́дешь, да́льше бу́дешь, the slower you go, the further you'll get. The latter is often translated passively, e.g. как его́ зову́т?, what is his name? (lit. "how do they call him?"); ско́ро откро́ют две́ри, the doors will soon be opened ("they'll open the doors soon"). N.B. that the pronoun они́, unlike the English "they," is used only with reference to definite people. Note again the use of the negative second person singular perfective in the meaning "you (one) can't": его́ фами́лию не вы́говоришь, you can't pronounce his last name.

B. Infinitive. With the dative, this can imply a kind of obligation or necessity, e.g. что нам де́лать? what are we to do, what should we do?; кому́ идти́? who is (supposed) to go?; ему́ идти́, he is to go. These expressions are somewhat weaker than those of necessity with на́до (ну́жно). Note also the construction "there is someone (to): есть кому́ plus the infinitive, e.g. есть (бы́ло, бу́дет) кому́ убира́ть ко́мнату, there is (was, will be) someone to clean up the room. But when "someone" is an object, it must of course go into the case demanded, e.g. у неё есть с кем говори́ть, there is someone for her to talk with.

C. Third Person Singular/Neuter Past. This is the most frequent type of subjectless, impersonal verb. The verbs сле́дует (сле́довало) and прихо́дится (пришло́сь, придётся) can be used as synonyms of на́до (ну́жно) with the dative, but have the special meanings, respectively, of "it is fitting, one should" and "one has occasion to": e.g.

вам сле́дует бо́льше занима́ться, you should study more; мне пришло́сь поговори́ть с ним, I had to talk with him (or "I had occasion to...", depending on context). Note also удаётся (удало́сь, уда́стся) succeed in, manage to: ему́ не удало́сь реши́ть зада́чу, he didn't succeed in solving (manage to solve) the problem.

For the usage of other reflexive verbs in impersonal contexts, notably ка́жется and хо́чется, review 40E. Here it may be noted that the reflexive forms of many common verbs, e.g. спи́тся, sleep; пи́шется, write, are used, most often in negative contexts, as colloquial equivalents of (не) мочь plus infinitive, e.g. сего́дня мне не пи́шется (писа́лось), I can't (couldn't) write today (although for no definite, tangible reason).

The verb нра́виться, to be pleasing, appeal to, is not strictly speaking impersonal, since it must agree with the grammatical subject (i.e., what is pleasing), e.g. мне нра́вится э́та карти́на (нра́вятся э́ти карти́ны), I like this picture (these pictures). The perfective понра́виться implies to be pleasing immediately, at first glance, and remain so. The verb люби́ть implies more than a surface or initial attraction, and one of longer standing. With verbs especially, люби́ть and not нра́виться is used, e.g. я люблю́ танцева́ть, I like to dance. The perfective полюби́ть means "get to like, love."

Certain natural phenomena are expressed by the third (neuter) singular, e.g. темне́ет, it is getting dark; здесь ду́ет, there is a draft here (lit. "it blows here"); в э́той ко́мнате па́хнет цвета́ми, there is a smell of flowers in this room. If a person is involved, this becomes the direct object of the impersonal verb, e.g. его́ уби́ло мо́лнией, he was killed by lightning (lit. "it killed him with lightning"). This construction is also used for certain things involving the body, usually of an unpleasant nature, e.g. её рва́ло, she was vomiting. But note у меня́ боли́т голова́ (боля́т но́ги) my head aches (legs ache), where the verb, although used only in the third person, has a singular or plural subject it must agree with.

Note the use of нет (не́ было, не бу́дет) with a personal subject, which becomes genitive: он был на уро́ке, he was at the lesson; but его́ не́ было на уро́ке, he wasn't at the lesson. However, if it is stated that the subject is somewhere else: он не́ был на уро́ке, а в кино́, He was not at the lesson, but at the movies.

Exercises. Oral Drills: 1. Combine subjects, verbs and objects appropriately in present and past, declining and conjugating as necessary: I. Я, он, она́, мы, они́ II. люби́ть, (по)нра́виться III. де́ти, Ни́на, игра́ть в те́ннис, э́тот фильм, э́ти пла́тья

2. Make affirmative and negative sentences in present, past and future: I. Я, он, Соколов, Анна, мы, девушки II. дома, здесь, на собрании, у профессора

Translate: 1. It can't be helped--you'll never get this window open. 2. What's your name? And what's your last name? 3. I was told that Myshkin was dead. 4. What was I supposed to say? 5. Who could I ask about it? 6. I had nothing to say and nobody to ask. 7. But now there is somebody to ask. 8. And there is somebody to tell me what to do. 9. Yesterday I had to buy Tanya a present. 10. She is getting married to Sergey, although I always told her she should marry me. 11. I wonder if she'll manage to be happy with him. 12. I don't like the apartment they're going to live in. 13. There is a smell of old wood in it. 14. But Tanya said she liked the furniture. 15. When I was there last week there was a draft under the door. 16. Because of that, I couldn't sit still. 17. Later I had a headache and a sore throat and couldn't get to sleep. 18. I called this morning, but Tanya wasn't there. 19. She must have been at Sergey's. 20. I don't think I like Sergey.

54. TRANSLATION OF "TO BE"

A. Быть and Related Verbs. Although the present tense of "to be" is normally not expressed, the lack of a linking verb in Russian is often felt and the connecting "blank" filled in. Есть, the only remaining present form of быть in addition to its normal meaning of "there is, are" when stressing the existence of something, serves as an **emphatic** "am, is, are", e.g., он был чемпион, он (и) есть чемпион, he was the champion, he still _is_ the champion; я хочу знать людей, как они есть, I want to know people as they _are_. It is found in enumerations such as весенние месяцы есть: апрель, май, июнь the spring months are April, May, and June; and is obligatory when subject and predicate nominative are the same, e.g. правда есть правда, truth is truth.

The verb бывать has the meaning "to be habitually" and is related to быть in much the same way as an indefinite is related to a definite verb of motion (cf. 39B). It, however, has a present tense which is used as often as the past, e.g., он бывает в Нью Йорке по средам, he is in New York on Wednesdays.

B. Verbs Requiring an Instrumental Predicate. For verbs such as казаться, seem to be; становиться/стать, become; оставаться/остаться, remain; оказываться/оказаться, turn out to be, all close in meaning to the basic linking verb, see 27B. Являться, lit. "appear to be" and представлять собой, lit. "represent oneself to be" are often found in definition-type sentences, e.g. ястреб является хищной

птицей (or представляет собой хищную птицу) the hawk is
a bird of prey.

C. Verbs of Position. The English "be" is often made
more specific by the usage of verbs such as the following:
находиться, be located; стоять, be standing; сидеть, be
sitting; лежать, be lying, e.g. где находится библиотека?
where is the library?; телевизор стоит в углу, the tele-
vision set is in the corner (note also стоять в коленях,
to be kneeling); газеты лежат на столе, the papers are on
the table; город Сент-Луис стоит (лежит) на Миссисипи,
the city of St. Louis is on the Mississippi. Often there
is a sense of idleness or helplessness, e.g. он теперь
сидит в тюрьме, he is in jail now; он лежит в постели,
he is (staying) in bed (possibly because of laziness or
illness).

Exercises. Translate: 1. Dear Tanya: I have been here
in the hospital almost a month. 2. It is not bad here.
3. The hospital is on the river, surrounded by green
trees, and there are kind people around me. 4. The doctor says I can go home tomorrow, but I'll have to stay at
home for another month or two. 5. This will be hard for
me. 6. You remember how we used to be in Paris once a
month. 7. And now, I have turned out to be an invalid
(use инвалид). 8. What is an invalid? 9. The word, of
course, is in the dictionary: "An invalid is a person who
cannot work." 10. But at the same time I remain your
good friend. 11. Think of me not as I was, but as I am.
12. Hoping that you can do this, I am on my knees before
you. 13. P.S. I am worried about one thing: my car has
been on the street for a month now. 14. Please let me
know if it is still there, and if so, whether it is O.K.

GENERAL SUMMARY EXERCISE. There are mistakes in each of
the following sentences. Correct them:
1. Я говорил с товарищом о русских фильмах. 2. В декабри
секретарь работала в этом комнате. 3. Мой деньги лежит
там на столе. 4. Я сидел на береге и думал о моём саду.
5. У брата семь карандашов. 6. Американцы покупают много
кресл. 7. Эти Англичанины хорошо знают американские гор-
оды. 8. Три детей входили в магазине, когда встретили
матери. 9. Он держает эти пластинки, потому что он инте-
ресовается музыкой Чайковския. 10. Почему девочка плакает?
11. Я познакомю тебя с ней. 12. Они встают в семь часов.
13. Это случилось в городе Москвы. 14. Мы долго говорили
об Японском языке. 15. Почему он всё время смотрется на
этой девушке? 16. Мы встретились в вокзале и поспешили
дома. 17. Они ночевали в Николая доме. 18. Ричард Грант--
мой русский учитель. 19. Он не инженера, а механик. 20.
В этой комнате было нет стульев. 21. Я пошёл к магазину
купить новое платье. 22. Профессор учит Филиппу биологию.

23. Я прочитал мою статью к учителю, и когда я спросил его что он думал, он не ответил меня. 24. Они рубят дрова с топором. 25. Он долго искал для хорошей машины. 26. Я всегда говорил, что Роберт станет хорошего адвоката. 27. Варя готовит обед, и Ваня слушает на музыку. 28. Вы знаете если Соколов живёт в городе? 29. Я хочу жить только где живут добрне люди. 30. Мы смотрел на телевизор для некоторое время, тогда пошли в Николая. 31. Я люблю есть мороженое очень много. 32. После Маша сьела, она легла спать. 33. Этот ваш стол? Оно так большой! 34. Сегодня она чувствуется хорошая. 35. Смайли ударил моё плечо и крикнул, "Я разобью вашу голову!" 36. Кто было на собрание этим вечером? 37. Я не вижу здесь человека, который я пригласил. 38. Все знает, что трудно говорить по-русский. 39. Вы знаете это себя. 40. Мы часто учимся с друг другом. 41. Я никогда пишу кому-нибудь. 42. У меня ничего о чём говорить. 43. Мы думали, что вы не любили играть карты. 44. Если он приходит здесь, я скажу его. 45. Пётр почитал журнали всё утро. 46. Она кончила объяснить теорию. 47. Отец сказал с профессором о своём сынове. 48. Как часто вы идёте на библиотеке? 49. Мы идём в Нью Йорк один раз в месяц. 50. Он подходил меня и говорил мне, что он потерял его жену. 51. Спектакль начинает ровно в 8:00. Когда оно кончает? 52. Мне казался, что в этой комнате оно было холодно. 53. Смирнов сидел в неправильный стул. 54. "Закрывайте дверь", Нина сказала её дочери. 55. Давайте написать учителью. 56. Пусть он идти в работу пешком. 57. Если бы я целоваю её, она давает бы мне пощёчину. 58. Я хочу его остать меня в покое. 59. Куря папиросу, Сергей плавал в озере. 60. Мы говорили с писателем, написанный книгу, которая мы только что прочитали. 61. Иван теперь готовый к экзамену. 62. Это красивее цветок, чем тот. 63. Это платье дорогее того на семь доллара. 64. У меня больший дом, чем вы. 65. У Светлова пятьдесят один костюмов. 66. Павел приедет в будущую неделю. 67. Каждым летом мы ездим в деревню две или три недели. 68. Ивану не можно был играть на улицу. 69. Ему должен будет убирать комнату. 70. Сегодня Таня не на русском классе.

I. THE NOUN

A. Masculine   Singular

	Hard	Soft	Soft	Soft
N	заво́д	рубль	слу́чай	ге́ний
A	заво́д	рубль	слу́чай	ге́ния
G	заво́да	рубля́	слу́чая	ге́ния
P	заво́де	рубле́	слу́чае	ге́нии
D	заво́ду	рублю́	слу́чаю	ге́нию
I	заво́дом	рублём	слу́чаем	ге́нием

Plural

N	заво́ды	рубли́	слу́чаи	ге́нии
A	заво́ды	рубли́	слу́чаи	ге́ниев
G	заво́дов	рубле́й	слу́чаев	ге́ниев
P	заво́дах	рубля́х	слу́чаях	ге́ниях
D	заво́дам	рубля́м	слу́чаям	ге́ниям
I	заво́дами	рубля́ми	слу́чаями	ге́ниями

B. Neuter   Singular

N	де́ло	ружьё	зда́ние	и́мя
A	де́ло	ружьё	зда́ние	и́мя
G	де́ла	ружья́	зда́ния	и́мени
P	де́ле	ружье́	зда́нии	и́мени
D	де́лу	ружью́	зда́нию	и́мени
I	де́лом	ружьём	зда́нием	и́менем

Plural

N	дела́	ру́жья	зда́ния	имена́
A	дела́	ру́жья	зда́ния	имена́
G	дел	ру́жей	зда́ний	имён
P	дела́х	ру́жьях	зда́ниях	имена́х
D	дела́м	ру́жьям	зда́ниям	имена́м
I	дела́ми	ру́жьями	зда́ниями	имена́ми

Note: for **animate** nouns, such as ге́ний, the accusative is like the **genitive**. Otherwise, it is like the nominative.

C. <u>Feminine</u>

Singular

	Hard	Soft	Soft	Soft
N	ла́мпа	неде́ля	ле́кция	дверь
A	ла́мпу	неде́лю	ле́кцию	дверь
G	ла́мпы	неде́ли	ле́кции	две́ри
P	ла́мпе	неде́ле	ле́кции	две́ри
D	ла́мпе	неде́ле	ле́кции	две́ри
I	ла́мпой(-ою)	неде́лей(-ею)	ле́кцией(-ею)	две́рью

Plural

N	ла́мпы	неде́ли	ле́кции	две́ри
A	ла́мпы	неде́ли	ле́кции	две́ри
G	ламп	неде́ль	ле́кций	двере́й
P	ла́мпах	неде́лях	ле́кциях	дверя́х
D	ла́мпам	неде́лям	ле́кциям	дверя́м
I	ла́мпами	неде́лями	ле́кциями	дверя́ми

*Note: here and elsewhere in the feminine instrumental singular of nouns, adjectives and pronouns, the variant ending -ою (ею) is in general considered archaic or bookish, but is often used for stylistic or rhythmic purposes.

D. <u>Russian Family Names</u>

	Masculine	Feminine	Plural
N	Кузнецо́в	Кузнецо́ва	Кузнецо́вы
A	Кузнецо́ва	Кузнецо́ву	Кузнецо́вых
G	Кузнецо́ва	Кузнецо́вой	Кузнецо́вых
P	Кузнецо́ве	Кузнецо́вой	Кузнецо́вых
D	Кузнецо́ву	Кузнецо́вой	Кузнецо́вым
I	Кузнецо́вым	Кузнецо́вой	Кузнецо́выми

Note that this declension is partly nominal (masculine except instrumental, feminine nominative and accusative, and nominative plural) and partly adjectival (masculine instrumental, feminine except nominative and accusative, and plural except nominative). Similarly declined are names in -ев (ёв) and -ин (нн after ц). Names which are adjectival in form, e.g. Достое́вский, Толсто́й, are declined like adjectives throughout.

The general tendency is not to decline names with other endings. Those with consonantal endings (except -ых or -их) are declined like nouns when they refer to males only; names ending in vowels (except those in -а or -я, which are normally declined like feminine nouns) are not declined. The same principles are true of foreign names.

A. Hard

	Masculine	Neuter	Feminine	Plural
N	ва́жный	ва́жное	ва́жная	ва́жные
A	ва́жный/ого	ва́жное	ва́жную	ва́жные/ых
G	ва́жного	ва́жного	ва́жной	ва́жных
P	ва́жном	ва́жном	ва́жной	ва́жных
D	ва́жному	ва́жному	ва́жной	ва́жным
I	ва́жным	ва́жным	ва́жной(-ою)	ва́жными

Short Forms: ва́жен, важна́, ва́жно, ва́жны

B. Mixed: Stems in г, к, х

	Masculine	Neuter	Feminine	Plural
N	ру́сский	ру́сское	ру́сская	ру́сские
A	ру́сский/ого	ру́сское	ру́сскую	ру́сские/их
G	ру́сского	ру́сского	ру́сской	ру́сских
P	ру́сском	ру́сском	ру́сской	ру́сских
D	ру́сскому	ру́сскому	ру́сской	ру́сским
I	ру́сским	ру́сским	ру́сской(-ою)	ру́сскими

Mixed: Stems in ж, ч, ш, щ

N	хоро́ший	хоро́шее	хоро́шая	хоро́шие
A	хоро́ший/его	хоро́шее	хоро́шую	хоро́шие/их
G	хоро́шего	хоро́шего	хоро́шей	хоро́ших
P	хоро́шем	хоро́шем	хоро́шей	хоро́ших
D	хоро́шему	хоро́шему	хоро́шей	хоро́шим
I	хоро́шим	хоро́шим	хоро́шей(-ею)	хоро́шими

Short Forms: хоро́ш, хороша́, хорошо́, хороши́

N.B. when the endings of "sibilant" stems are **stressed**, о appears instead of е: большо́й, большо́го, etc.

C. Soft (in -ний only)

N	си́ний	си́нее	си́няя	си́ние
A	си́ний/его	си́нее	си́нюю	си́ние/их
G	си́него	си́него	си́ней	си́них
P	си́нем	си́нем	си́ней	си́них
D	си́нему	си́нему	си́ней	си́ним
I	си́ним	си́ним	си́ней(-ею)	си́ними

Short Forms: синь, синя́, си́не, си́ни

D. <u>Relative</u> (derived chiefly from names of animals)

	Masculine	Neuter	Feminine	Plural
N	коро́вий	коро́вье	коро́вья	коро́вьи
A	коро́вий/ьего	коро́вье	коро́вью	коро́вьи/ьих
G	коро́вьего	коро́вьего	коро́вьей	коро́вьих
P	коро́вьем	коро́вьем	коро́вьей	коро́вьих
D	коро́вьему	коро́вьему	коро́вьей	коро́вьим
I	коро́вьим	коро́вьим	коро́вьей(ьею)	коро́вьими

(Compare the declensions of чей, whose, and тре́тий, third)

E. <u>Possessive</u> (derived from nouns referring to people or from diminutives of first names)

N	ма́мин	ма́мино	ма́мина	ма́мины
A	ма́мин/а(ого)	ма́мино	ма́мину	ма́мины/ых
G	ма́мина(-ого)	ма́мина(-ого)	ма́миной	ма́миных
P	ма́мином	ма́мином	ма́миной	ма́миных
D	ма́мину(-ому)	ма́мину(-ому)	ма́миной	ма́миным
I	ма́миным	ма́миным	ма́миной(-ою)	ма́миными

Note: the longer masculine endings are used more often in literature.

III. PRONOUNS

A. <u>Personal</u>

			Singular		(Reflexive)
N	я	ты	он; оно́	она́	--
A	меня́	тебя́	его́	её	себя́
G	меня́	тебя́	его́	её	себя́
P	мне	тебе́	нём	ней	себе́
D	мне	тебе́	ему́	ей	себе́
I	мной(бю)	тобо́й(бю)	им	ей(ею)	собо́й(бю)

		Plural		(Interrogative)	
N	мы	вы	они́	кто	что
A	нас	вас	их	кого́	что
G	нас	вас	их	кого́	чего́
P	нас	вас	них	ком	чём
D	нам	вам	им	кому́	чему́
I	на́ми	ва́ми	и́ми	кем	чем

N.B. in third person personal pronouns, н appears after a preposition, e.g. у него́, к ней, о них

	Masculine	Neuter	Feminine	Plural
N	мой	моё	моя́	мои́
A	мой/моего́	моё	мою́	мои́/мои́х
G	моего́	моего́	мое́й	мои́х
P	моём	моём	мое́й	мои́х
D	моему́	моему́	мое́й	мои́м
I	мои́м	мои́м	мое́й(-е́ю)	мои́ми
N	наш	на́ше	на́ша	на́ши
A	наш/на́шего	на́ше	на́шу	на́ши/на́ших
G	на́шего	на́шего	на́шей	на́ших
P	на́шем	на́шем	на́шей	на́ших
D	на́шему	на́шему	на́шей	на́шим
I	на́шим	на́шим	на́шей(-ею)	на́шими

Declined like мой are твой and свой. Like наш is ваш.
The third person possessives его́, её, их are indeclinable
(being the genitive forms of the personal pronouns). N.B.
that unlike the personal pronouns, they do **not** take the
н after prepositions.

(Interrogative)

N	чей	чьё	чья	чьи
A	чей/чьего́	чьё	чью	чьи/чьих
G	чьего́	чьего́	чьей	чьих
P	чьём	чьём	чьей	чьих
D	чьему́	чьему́	чьей	чьим
I	чьим	чьим	чьей(-е́ю)	чьи́ми

The archaic interrogative-relative pronoun кой, whose
(which in the singular appears only in the oblique cases:
ко́его, ко́ему, etc.) is declined like мой; кото́рый, which,
who, has an **adjectival** declension (as in IIA).

Also like adjectives of type IIA are ино́й, other; ка́ждый,
each (one); са́мый, same. Like adjectives of IIB with
stems in velars (г, к) are друго́й, other; мно́гие, many;
вся́кий, every (one); како́й, what; тако́й, such.

C. Demonstrative and Definite

	Masculine	Neuter	Feminine	Plural
N	э́тот	э́то	э́та	э́ти
A	э́тот/э́того	э́то	э́ту	э́ти/э́тих
G	э́того	э́того	э́той	э́тих
P	э́том	э́том	э́той	э́тих
D	э́тому	э́тому	э́той	э́тим
I	э́тим	э́тим	э́той(-ою)	э́тими

N	тот	то	та	те
A	тот/того́	то	ту	те/тех
G	того́	того́	той	тех
P	том	том	той	тех
D	тому́	тому́	той	тем
I	тем	тем	той(-ою)	те́ми

N	сам	само́	сама́	са́ми
A	сам/самого́	само́	саму́(само́ё)	са́ми/сами́х
G	самого́	самого́	само́й	сами́х
P	само́м	само́м	само́й	сами́х
D	самому́	самому́	само́й	сами́м
I	сами́м	сами́м	само́й(-бю)	сами́ми

(the form само́ё is considered archaic or bookish)

N	весь	всё	вся	все
A	весь/всего́	всё	всю	все/всех
G	всего́	всего́	всей	всех
P	всём	всём	всей	всех
D	всему́	всему́	всей	всем
I	всем	всем	всей(-бю)	все́ми

D. **Negative Pronouns.** The chief thing to remember about pronouns like никто́ and ничто́ is that when they are declined with prepositions, the preposition separates the negative particle and the pronoun, making three written elements in all, e.g. ни у кого́, ни о чём, etc.

(Similarly declined is the reciprocal pronoun друг дру́га: друг к дру́гу, друг с дру́гом, etc.)

A. Cardinals

	Masculine	Neuter	Feminine	Plural
N	оди́н	одно́	одна́	одни́
A	оди́н/одного́	одно́	одну́	одни́/одни́х
G	одного́	одного́	одно́й	одни́х
P	одно́м	одно́м	одно́й	одни́х
D	одному́	одному́	одно́й	одни́м
I	одни́м	одни́м	одно́й(-бю)	одни́ми

(Two, three, four, five)

N	два; две	три	четы́ре	пять
A	два,две/двух	три/трёх	четыре/ёх	пять
G	двух	трёх	четырёх	пяти́
P	двух	трёх	четырёх	пяти́
D	двум	трём	четырём	пяти́
I	двумя́	тремя́	четырьмя́	пятью́

The special form две is used for the feminine nominative-accusative. Declined like пять are the numerals 6-20 and 30, except that 11-19 do not have stressed endings but retain the stress of the nominative: шесть, семь, во́семь, де́вять, де́сять, оди́ннадцать, двена́дцать, трина́дцать, четы́рнадцать, пятна́дцать, шестна́дцать, семна́дцать, восемна́дцать, девятна́дцать, два́дцать; три́дцать

(Forty through one hundred)

N	со́рок	пятьдеся́т	девяно́сто	сто
A	со́рок	пятьдеся́т	девяно́сто	сто
G	сорока́	пяти́десяти	девяно́ста	ста
P	сорока́	пяти́десяти	девяно́ста	ста
D	сорока́	пяти́десяти	девяно́ста	ста
I	сорока́	пятью́десятью	девяно́ста	ста

Declined like пятьдеся́т are 60, 70, and 80 (шестьдеся́т, се́мьдеся́т, во́семьдеся́т).

(Two hundred through nine hundred)

N	две́сти	три́ста	пятьсо́т
A	две́сти	три́ста	пятьсо́т
G	двухсо́т	трёхсо́т	пятисо́т
P	двухста́х	трёхста́х	пятиста́х
D	двумста́м	трёмста́м	пятиста́м
I	двумяста́ми	тремяста́ми	пятьюста́ми

Note that here, as with 50 through 80, <u>both</u> parts of the numeral are declined. Тысяча, thousand, and миллион, million, are nouns and declined as such in singular and plural, except that тысяча has the instrumental singular тысячью.

("Both" and "one and a half")

N	óба	óбе	полторá, полторы́
A	óба/обóих	óбе/обéих	полторá, полторы́
G	обóих	обéих	полу́тора
P	обóих	обéих	полу́тора
D	обóим	обéим	полу́тора
I	обóими	обéими	полу́тора

B. Collectives and Adverbs of Quantity

N	двóе	чéтверо	мнóго
A	двóе/двойх	чéтверо/четверы́х	мнóго
G	двойх	четверы́х	мнóгих
P	двойх	четверы́х	мнóгих
D	двойм	четверы́м	мнóгим
I	двойми	четверы́ми	мнóгими

Declined like двóе is трóе; like чéтверо are пятеро, шéстеро, сéмеро, вóсьмеро, дéвятеро, дéсятеро. Like мнóго are скóлько, немнóго, нéсколько.

C. <u>Ordinals</u> from one to ten are as follows: пéрвый, вторóй, трéтий, четвёртый, пя́тый, шестóй, седьмóй, восьмóй, девя́тый, деся́тый. Eleven through nineteen are formed from the cardinals with -тый, with no change of stress: одúннадцатый, двенáдцатый, etc. The tens from 20 to 100 are: двадцáтый, тридцáтый, сороковóй, пятидеся́тый, шестидеся́тый, семидеся́тый, восьмидеся́тый, девянóстый, сóтый. The following hundreds are formed with the <u>genitive</u> of the cardinal plus -сотый: двухсóтый, трёхсóтый, etc. "Thousandth" is тысячный; "millionth" миллиóнный. All are declined like hard stem <u>adjectives</u>, with the exception of трéтий, third, which is declined like a "relative" adjective (see IID).

Only the final element of compound ordinal numerals has the ordinal ending, e.g. двáдцать пéрвый, twenty-first; трúста шестьдеся́т пя́тый, three hundred sixty-fifth.

A. <u>Conjugation I</u>   (Imperfective)   (Perfective)

Infinitive		чита́ть	рисова́ть	верну́ть

Present				
	я	чита́ю	рису́ю	верну́
	ты	чита́ешь	рису́ешь	вернёшь
	он	чита́ет	рису́ет	вернёт
	мы	чита́ем	рису́ем	вернём
	вы	чита́ете	рису́ете	вернёте
	они́	чита́ют	рису́ют	верну́т

Past Masc.	чита́л	рисова́л	верну́л
Fem.	чита́ла	рисова́ла	верну́ла
Neut.	чита́ло	рисова́ло	верну́ло
Pl.	чита́ли	рисова́ли	верну́ли

Future	бу́ду			(For perfectives,
	бу́дешь			"present tense"
	бу́дет	чита́ть	рисова́ть	forms have
	бу́дем			future meaning)
	бу́дете			
	бу́дут			

Imperative	чита́й(те)	рису́й(те)	верни́(те)
Pres Gerund	чита́я	рису́я	--
Past Gerund	-чита́в(ши)	-рисова́в(ши)	верну́в(ши)
Pres Act Part	чита́ющий	рису́ющий	--
Pres Pass Part	чита́емый	рису́емый	--
Past Act Part	чита́вший	рисова́вший	верну́вший
Past Pass Part	-чи́танный	-рисо́ванный	вёрнутый

The <u>conditional</u> is formed with the past tense and the
particle бы, e.g. я чита́л бы, он чита́л бы, она́ чита́ла
бы, мы чита́ли бы, они чита́ли бы

The <u>passive voice</u> is formed with any tense of "to be"
plus the short forms of the present or past passive
participle, e.g. кни́га чита́ема, кни́га была́ чита́ема;
кни́га вёрнута, кни́га была вёрнута, кни́га бу́дет вёрнута

(The hyphen before the past gerund and past passive participle indicates that these are normally formed only
from perfectives.)

B. <u>Conjugation II</u>

	(Imperfective)	(Perfective)	(Reflexive)
Infinitive	спо́рить	положи́ть	моли́ться

Present

я	спо́рю	положу́	молю́сь
ты	спо́ришь	поло́жишь	мо́лишься
он	спо́рит	поло́жит	мо́лится
мы	спо́рим	поло́жим	мо́лимся
вы	спо́рите	поло́жите	мо́литесь
они́	спо́рят	поло́жат	мо́лятся

Past Masc.

Masc.	спо́рил	положи́л	моли́лся
Fem.	спо́рила	положи́ла	моли́лась
Neut.	спо́рило	положи́ло	моли́лось
Pl.	спо́рили	положи́ли	моли́лись

Future

бу́ду
бу́дешь
бу́дет спо́рить (For perfectives,
бу́дем "present tense" моли́ться
бу́дете forms have
бу́дут future meaning)

Imperative	спо́рь(те)	положи́(те)	моли́сь (моли́тесь)
Pres Gerund	спо́ря	--	моля́сь
Past Gerund	-спо́рив(ши)	положи́в(ши)	-моли́вшись
Pres Act Part	спо́рящий	--	мо́лящийся
Pres Pass Part	--	--	--
Past Act Part	спо́ривший	положи́вший	моли́вшийся
Past Pass Part	--	поло́женный	--

<u>Reflexives</u> do not have passive participles. Perfectives
do not have present participles or gerunds.